Surgical Sensation at St. Sennapod's

or

Dr Scalpel's Missing Bit

John Gardiner
and
Fiz Coleman

Music arranged by James Pearson

Samuel French — London

New York — Sydney — Toronto — Hollywood

CHARACTERS

Miss Crisp, receptionist at St Sennapod's Hospital
Jim Pill, male nurse
Miss Clamp, Matron at St Sennapod's Hospital
Lint, Administrator
Dr Boldly, junior doctor on the staff of St Sennapod's Hospital
Nurse Bright SRN, a nurse
Dr Scalpel, a sinister doctor
Tootski, his assistant
Doris Bucket, a patient with her foot stuck in a bucket
George Flower, a patient with a watering can stuck on his head
Kenneth Kipper, a patient with a kipper stuck down his throat
Nurse Cuddle SRN, a nurse
Sir Barnaby Booth-Barrington, leading surgeon
Fred Bunch, (Inspector Nab in disguise)
Nurse 1/Mrs Gigglesworth/Midwife
Nurse 2/Mr Glum/Vicar
Nurse 3/Mrs Nervy

Other nurses and ancillary staff can be included

The action of the play takes place in Ward 10 of St Sennapod's Hospital

MUSICAL NUMBERS

ACT I

Song 1	St Sennapod's At Your Service	Company
Song 2	Tuesday, Tonsils and You	Boldly, Bright
Song 3	Anthem to Sir Barnaby	Company
Song 4	Nickin' Bits in the Night	Scalpel, Tootski
Song 5	I've Left My Gloves In	Boldly, Company

ACT II

Song 6	Come to My 'Lotment	George, Doris
Song 7	We've Got A Nasty Job To Do	Jim
Song 8	Thank You Everyone	Company

The music for these songs can be found at the end of the text

PRODUCTION NOTES

Characters and their costumes

Miss Crisp—the receptionist. She is prim and proper yet despite her outward prudish nature she has a heart of gold. She is quite vulnerable beneath the over-scrupulous veneer. She does not wear a white coat but a dark two-piece tailored suit—smart but severe, pure white high-collared blouse and glasses hanging on a necklace. Her hair is swept up into a refined hygienic bun. Originally performed with a puritanical Scottish accent.

Jim Pill—a male nurse. The audience should really identify with him. Funny, quick and inventive. Full of comic business and cockney cheek. He wears a white male nurse's tunic over shirt plus plain trousers and shoes.

Matron—Miss Clamp. A huge-bosomed mammoth. The archetypal "Carry on Matron" always sweeping into wards and surgeries in full sail with all guns blasting. A deep-voiced authoritarian who makes Boadicea look like Olive Oyl. She wears the old-fashioned blue tunic and starched head-dress of a stock matron with dark stockings, sensible shoes and watch.

Lint—a slimy, slippery, snake-like administrator. Comic because he is so despicably oily. On stage he seems to be anatomically attached to Matron. He is physically always close to her (suddenly appearing behind her, peering over her shoulder or creeping between her legs). He has a revolting, snickery, nasal, pig-like sort of laugh. A leech with black slicked-back hair, a suspicion of bad teeth and bad breath. Hundreds of biros in the top pocket of his white but soiled coat. A clipboard, shabby shoes and creased trousers.

Nurse Bright—a pretty Mills and Boon heroine. She adores Dr Boldly, the nursing profession, clean sheets, lame dogs, handicapped hamsters, etc. Wears straight SRN uniform with some illegal decorative and alluring additions. A voice like a girl in a shampoo advert.

Dr Boldly—outwardly a Mills and Boon hero—handsome, assertive and decisive but inwardly quite gauche, insecure and limp. He has a host of pipes that he stuffs in his mouth throughout the performance which he thinks gives him a "macho" quality. White coat over an executive three-piece suit.

Dr Scalpel—a creepy Klaus Kinski type—mittel-European practitioner, almost certainly unqualified. Quite frightening and sinister. Moves in a panther-like manner but suddenly galvanized by violent and grotesque neural spasms. Quite clearly not all there. He wears a dishevelled suit that bears a suggestion of past respectability.

Tootski—Scalpel's assistant. A surgical mistake. Heavily bandaged and stitched. Head and body swathed in crêpe bandages. He/she has one gigantic transplanted foot (see notes on page 39). The audience must feel some sympathy for this character. He/she has a bloodied and soiled white coat which covers most of the anatomical error. Funny not horrific.

Doris Bucket (a patient)—a lovable cheerful working-class lady, "the salt of the earth". Always on the look-out for a new husband. She wears a large crossover apron, Nora Batty stockings, flat-soled shoes and a headscarf. Foot stuck in a bucket.

George Flower (a patient)—a kind of human flower-pot man. Genial and rustic with costume to reflect such a nature. A watering can stuck on his head.

Nurse Cuddle—a pretty nurse with warm outgoing tendencies towards male patients. Standard SRN uniform.

Kenneth Kipper—an ordinary bloke on the look-out for pretty nurses with warm outgoing tendencies towards male patients. He has difficulty in speaking as a kipper protrudes from his mouth. Colourful underpants, string vest, boots, loud socks, trousers, shirt, jumper, mac and flat cap.

Sir Barnaby Booth-Barrington—Old Etonian. Cut-glass accent. Immaculate three-piece or morning suit. The best surgeon since Dr Kildare. Monocle.

Fred Bunch—a neurotic who has lost his way as a visitor. Must give the impression that he has walked down every corridor in the hospital and is completely confused. Nervous, apprehensive but constantly curious about hospital activities. Old mackintosh, trilby. Really **Inspector Nab** in disguise.

Nurse 1/Mrs Gigglesworth—as Mrs G.—a dotty old eccentric, brightly-coloured clothes and hat—she can't stop giggling.

Nurse 2/Mr Glum/Vicar—as Mr Glum, a misery-guts, dresses in black, drab, monotone voice. A nutty, eccentric vicar.

Nurse 3/Mrs Nervy—as Mrs Nervy—a loony who twitches every limb—all at the same time.

The Set

The action of the whole play takes place in Ward 10 of St Sennapod's Hospital. L there is a lift marked "LIFT TO ALL FLOORS". DL is a large filing cabinet. LC is a large table upon which there is a small switchboard, telephone and reception paraphernalia. A small sign on the table reads "MISS CRISP—RECEPTION". Behind the table is a swivel chair. UC there is a cubicle for emergency patients to change. This is marked "EMERGENCY ADMISSIONS". The cubicle is curtained to the floor. There is access on and off at the rear of the cubicle. The rear window has a large window, draped, looking out on to gardens. UR are two hospital beds, with bedside lockers. The beds are raised at the head end in order to improve sight lines. Far UR is a large cupboard. DR is a round coffee table with four plastic chairs. This area is marked "RECEPTION AREA". There are exits L and R marked respectively "EXIT/STAIRS ONLY" and "EXIT". The ward is pleasantly decorated in cream paint. The curtains are bright and cheerful. The whole ward has been or will be decorated with paper chains and is generally festive as for a party.

Lighting and Effects

Lighting changes are minimal and the basic lighting which should be warm only changes for specials on Barnaby's Anthem, Boldly's Operation and Doris's and George's song. Night and mystery could use steel but atmosphere could be controlled just by fading on the master dimmer. Reference to changes appear in the script.

Music should be used throughout on a live piano, directors to use imagination and invention for required effect. Quite a number of suggestions have been made as to the mood required. Liberal use of the piano under the spoof scenes will colour the humour and action. Lift. A bell or better still one note on a large glockenspiel should be struck every time the lift door opens. There is a bellpush by the lift door which signals the sound. The door slides open one way ONLY, manually. Your lift operator can handle both sound and action.

ACT I

The play really starts with the following pre-show business:

Outside of the theatre:
Nurses and backstage crew are decorating the entrance, putting up signs advertising St Sennapod's Hospital party. (The party may celebrate Christmas, Easter, a reunion, an anniversary or just a party.) **George Flower** is arranging some flowers, watering or planting. They all talk to the audience as they arrive. "Welcome to St Sennapod's", "We're getting ready for the party", "Lovely weather ain't it", etc.

Foyer/Entrance
The audience are asked to present their appointment cards (tickets) to **Matron** and **Lint**. They are welcomed by **Miss Crisp**, **Dr Boldly** and **Nurse Bright**. **Miss Crisp** praises all the children for being so healthy, clean and tidy but remonstrates with and chastizes all adults for having grubby fingernails, uncleaned teeth, filthy necks etc. "They should be ashamed of themselves." **Dr Boldly** and **Nurse Bright** do brief medical check-ups on some children. They are all absolutely A1. "Perfect, absolutely perfect Susan!" "Yes, aren't they Stephen." **Lint** and **Matron** take appointment cards which will have name and address plus a lucky number written on each (see note on tickets on page 38). **Lint** and **Matron** also keep an eagle eye out for any dropped litter.

Foyer—Auditorium
Hospital muzak is playing. **Jim** and **Nurse Cuddle** act as couriers between Administration in the foyer and the activities in the auditorium. They guide the audience through to the auditorium and encourage them, especially children, to help with the decorations for the party.

Auditorium
The rest of the cast are getting ready for the party. All are asked to help putting up decorations, blowing up balloons, painting cut-outs and pictures to put up on the walls of the theatre and set. Have plenty of continuous jobs to do (get brushes, water-colour paints, crêpe paper, balloons, signs, wrapping paper for prizes etc.). **Doris**, without the bucket on her foot, is busy cleaning the auditorium seats and Hoovering the floor and doors. **Fred Bunch** periodically asks people the way to the surgery or dispensary etc. He is always making enquiries. All doors and exit doors in the auditorium are signposted "X-ray department", "Pathology", etc. and the cast use all these doors. **Sir Barnaby Booth-Barrington** is getting adults to fill in admission forms (see note on page 38).

The play starts on a given signal that **Miss Crisp** is coming! The cast usher the children to their seats with "Watch out, it's Miss Crisp, now we're for it. Quick get in your seat, she's an old fusspot."

Miss Crisp strides into the auditorium, up on to the stage and the Company assemble on stage

An electric buzzer sounds on the switchboard. The Company freeze, staring at Miss Crisp

Crisp (*to Company and audience*) Has anybody been messing about with this switchboard?
All No, Miss Crisp.
Crisp Are you absolutely sure of that?
All Yes, Miss Crisp.
Crisp Good! I will not tolerate people who try to pull out my plugs——

Someone makes a "pop" noise

—or fiddle with my phones.

Someone makes a "ring" noise

Is that quite clear?
All Yes, Miss Crisp.
Crisp I'm relieved to hear it. Good-morning children. Welcome to St Sennapod's Hospital. This is Reception and I am Miss Crisp. Have you all handed in your appointment cards? Excellent! Well. Let me introduce you to all the personnel that work at St Sennapod's. Sit up straight please . . . I'm going to sing.
All Oh no!

Song 1: St Sennapod's At Your Service

Crisp	St Sennapod's at your service St Sennapod's at your call
All (*hands to ears, shouting*) Hello!	
Crisp	St Sennapod's the hospital Where everyone's on the ball
All (*thumbs up*) That's us.	
Crisp	We like to cut off nasty bits

They snip scissors (mimed)

	We like to fight disease
All (*nodding*)	That's true.
Crisp (*moving*)	It's all part of the service Of St Sennapod's surgery.
All (*copying her moves*)	It's all part of the service Of St Sennapod's surgery.
Crisp	I'll introduce you personally To all our expert staff
All (*pointing up*)	The tops!
Crisp	Sir Barnaby Booth-Barrington A surgeon of real class.
All (*pointing to him*)	He's great.
Sir Barnaby	I'm off on one-month's holiday And left them with the key

He hands Crisp the key

All Hurrah!	
Sir Barnaby (*moving*)	To see that no-one comes to harm At St Sennapod's surgery.
All (*copying his moves*)	To see that no-one comes to harm At St Sennapod's surgery.
Crisp	Now please be quiet

They kneel

	And sit up straight It's Matron spick and span
All	Sit up!
Crisp	With vice-like grip and beady eye She'll catch you if she can

All Watch out!

  Matron sweeps in

Matron	Don't answer back or you will get Two enemas or three.
All Oh no!	
Matron (*moving*)	For that's the way you're kept in line At St Sennapod's surgery.

They stand and copy her moves

All	For that's the way we're kept in line At St Sennapod's surgery.

  Boldly enters

Boldly	Young Stephen Boldly is my name I'll stitch you up in time
All Yes please!	

  Nurse Bright enters

Bright	I'm Susan Bright who's by his side To make sure you'll be fine
All She's nice!	
Bright	We are in love and hope to wed

They hold hands

	As you can clearly see
All Aaah!	
Bright	Just some of the naughty things we do
	At St Sennapod's surgery
All (*copying them*)	Just some of the naughty things we do
	At St Sennapod's surgery.
Jim (*pushing to the front*)	Hallo! My name is young Jim Pill
	I love a joke you see
All Ay ay!	
Lint (*pushing to the front*)	And I am Lint the admin. man
	A nosy parker me
All Watch him!	
Jim }	We have to clean the pots and pans
Lint }	And keep the place germ-free
All Quite free.	
Jim } (*moving*)	Just some of the mucky jobs we do
Lint }	At St Sennapod's surgery
All (*copying them*)	Just some of the mucky jobs we do
	At St Sennapod's surgery.
	St Sennapod's at your service
	St Sennapod's at your call
	It's all part of the service
	At St Sennapod's surge . . .
	St Sennapod's surge . . .
	St Sennapod's surgery.

At the end of the song, the Company are grinning at the audience

Matron Don't stand there grinning inanely. (*She claps*)

The grins disappear

This hospital will not run itself. (*To the children*) Quite hopeless. Be about your business.

They go to task at speed

Sir Barnaby Long vacation!

He grabs his suitcase and exits

Boldly Operation!

He looks at his watch and exits

Lint Examination! (*He stands slimily, putting on his glasses*)
Bright Vaccination!

She exits, taking out a hypodermic

Crisp Communication! (*She points at the switchboard, then sits at the table*)
Jim Elevation! (*He points at the lift, then goes to it*)
Matron (*out front*) Searching for nasty smells! (*She sniffs, smells Lint*) Pooh! (*She takes out a spray and sprays him*)

Lint and Matron exit with the rest of the Company

As soon as she has gone, Jim steps out of the lift and talks to the audience

Jim This is the hospital lift, with yours truly Jim Pill in charge. This is the first floor see. Everybody arrives at the basement and then when Miss Crisp says——
Crisp (*speaking on the phone*) Reception. Miss Crisp speaking. Which department do you require?

Jim says it with her, mimicking

Jim —I pick 'em up and deliver them.
Crisp Emergency Admissions? Certainly, first floor. Please take the lift and report to Miss Crisp.

Jim repeats, sotto voce

Jim Ay ay the lift, that's me. Let's see what motley mob of nutcases we've got this morning.

Crisp is just bending down to get some folders from a cupboard; she has her back to Jim

Going down!

Crisp shoots up, she is alert to Jim's improprieties

Oops!

Jim goes into the lift and closes the doors. We hear a bell ring as the lift descends

Crisp Really! That young man has absolutely no sense of decorum. (*To the kids*) Now let me see. Emergency Admissions. They will need the necessary admission forms which must be completed correctly and returned for reference. Ah, here we are. (*She takes out forms from a folder*)

The bell rings and the lift doors open to reveal Jim

Jim First floor. Geriatrics, paediatrics, cuddly toys, camping equipment, old men's underwear——

A severe look from Crisp

—and Emergency Admissions. Here we go, my lovelies. You're gonna have fun today, Miss Crisp. Look at this first lot!

Mrs Gigglesworth, Glum and Nervy are crammed in the lift and they lean out and wave, then go back in

Crisp Oh goodness gracious me. How are we going to cope. We're so short-staffed with Sir Barnaby away.

The lift doors close

Jim Maybe some of these young gentlemen and lady doctors could help us. (*Signifying the children*)
Crisp Help us?
Jim Yeah. I reckon they know a lot about linctus, Lucozade—all that medical stuff.
Crisp Are you serious?
Jim Course I'm serious.
Crisp Well they all seem rather fidgetty to me.
Jim No I'm certain they could deal with any minor complaints.
Crisp Well we are terribly rushed off our feet.
Jim That's the ticket, Miss Crisp. If we introduce each patient maybe our assistants could suggest a lightning cure.

Nurse Cuddle enters, carrying a medical book

Cuddle Morning, Jim. What's the problem?
Crisp We're understaffed, Nurse Cuddle. Jim was wondering if these young people could assist us by suggesting cures for our emergency patients.
Cuddle I think that's a smashing idea.
Jim Would you help us, Nurse Cuddle?
Cuddle Of course, Jim. It's a pleasure.
Crisp (*finally convinced*) Excellent. (*To children*) All agreed? Thank you so much. Right. Call in the first victim . . . er . . . patient.

Jim brings in Mrs Gigglesworth. She giggles all the time

Jim Name please.
Mrs Gigglesworth (*she giggles as she speaks*) Mrs Gigglesworth.
Crisp Complaint?
Mrs Gigglesworth I can't stop . . . can't stop . . . giggling. It's so—(*she roars with laughter*)—embarrassing!

They all start giggling

Crisp Good heavens! Can anyone suggest a cure to stop Mrs Gigglesworth's giggles?

Whatever the children suggest as a cure, Jim, Miss Crisp and Nurse Cuddle carry it out making it as funny as possible, improvising. They should try a number of suggestions before one actually works

Jim That's it!
Crisp It's worked.
Cuddle Thank you very much. I'll jot that cure down in my medical book.
Mrs Gigglesworth (*very sensible and ungiggly now*) Thank you so much. I feel much more sensible now.

Nurse Cuddle shows her off

Mrs Gigglesworth exits

Jim Next patient please. (*To the audience*) I'm enjoying this.

The dead march is played funereally as Mr Glum enters

Crisp Name?

Mr Glum Mr Glum. (*He is the most miserable man ever seen*)
Jim Blimey—I can see his problem.
Cuddle ⎫
Crisp ⎭ (*together*) The miseries!
Jim Down in the dumps.
Mr Glum Cheesed off.
Cuddle ⎫
Crisp ⎭ (*together*) Oh dear. Oh dear. Oh dear.
Jim Blimey, we're all catching it.
Mr Glum No-one can make me laugh. I'm a moaning old misery-guts. There's no cure.
Jim If we could make him laugh that'd cure him?
Crisp Quite right, Jim. Now what could we do to make Mr Glum laugh?
Cuddle Any ideas please?

Again the children make a number of suggestions. Two or three are tried until he is cured and roars with laughter. Crisp, Cuddle and Jim are hysterical as well

Jim Oh dear, I'm aching.
Cuddle So funny!
Crisp Quite amusing, yes.
Mr Glum (*laughing*) That's great. Really terrific. I feel wonderful and so happy. (*To audience*) Thank you so much. I must find Mrs Gigglesworth and have a chat about old times.

   Mr Glum exits

Cuddle (*to the audience*) My, you are doing well. I think some of you should take this up professionally. (*Calling off*) Next please.

   Miss Nervy enters to wobbly piano music. She twitches all over

The Staff "mirror" the twitchings as if it is a slowly catching disease

Jim Bit more difficult this one.
Crisp Is it?
Jim Embarrassing really.
Crisp What seems to be the problem? Miss——?
Nervy Miss Nervy. (*She is like a mouse*)
Crisp What seems to be the problem, Miss Nervy?
Nervy (*very quietly so that they all have to close up round her*) Well . . . I've got a boil.
Jim ⎫
Cuddle ⎭ (*together; loudly*) A boil!
Crisp Shhh!
Nervy (*quieter*) On my bottie.
Jim ⎫
Cuddle ⎭ (*together*) On yer bottie!!!
Crisp Please be quiet—we must get to the bottom of this. (*She realizes the boob*) Oh I'm so sorry, Miss Nervy. Well children, how do we cure a—
All (*whispered*) Boil on the bottie.

The children suggest a cure and Miss Nervy is very relieved

Nervy I'll be able to sit down at last.

   Miss Nervy exits

Jim Well that's marvellous, Nurse Cuddle. All the minor problems dealt with.
Crisp Thank you all very much indeed.
Jim Now we come to the major surgery.
Crisp Very well. Wheel them in.
Cuddle I'll go and get new sheets for the beds.

   Fred enters holding a bunch of flowers

Fred Nurse, could you help me out?
Cuddle Certainly, which way did you come in?
Fred No, I don't want to "go out". I want to "come in" to see a friend. Make enquiries.
Cuddle This way please.

   Fred and Cuddle exit

Jim The patients for admission are just coming in the lift, Miss Crisp.
Crisp Excellent. Give me their names and complaints one by one please, Jim.

Jim Certainly, sir.

All the patients enter. They carry overnight bags

Kenneth Kipper. He said he swallowed a kipper and it stuck.

Kipper has a kipper tail protruding from his mouth. He grips the fish/head with his teeth when talking

Kipper Guy gallered git gand git guck. (I swallowed it . . . etc.)
Crisp Repulsive. Stand over there please.
Jim Doris Bucket.

Doris Bucket is a cleaning lady who has her foot stuck in a bucket. She clumps in. The actress can fix her own shoe in the bucket, the toe sticking out of the bottom to ease movement

She says she put her foot in it and it stuck.
Doris I put me foot in it and it stuck.
Crisp How clumsy! Over there.
Jim George Flower.

George is a nursery gardener and has a watering can rammed down over head. It has eye-holes cut in it. The top half is filled with water so that when he bends forward it wets anything in range

He says he had a row with the head gardener down the Garden Centre and he stuck this watering can over his head.
George I had a row with my head gardener down the Garden Centre and he stuck this watering can on me head.
Crisp Quite, quite ridiculous. Well come along quickly. Let's take down your particulars.

She looks sharply at Jim who has opened his mouth

Jim I never said a word. (*He helps Kipper across to Crisp*)
Crisp Full name?
Kipper Keggeth Kicker.
Crisp Kenneth Kipper. Folder, form, fill! (*She writes his name on a folder, hands it to him and points at the table where pencils are laid out*)
Kipper Kank koo.
Crisp Full name?
Doris Doris Bucket.
Crisp Folder, form, fill. (*She repeats the procedure as above with Kipper*)
Doris Thank you.
Crisp Full name?
George George Flower.
Crisp Folder, form, fill. (*She repeats the procedure*)
George Ta very much.
Jim That's the lot, Crispy.
Crisp Please, Mr Pill do not address me in that childish manner. My name is Miss Crisp. Now will you plea—— (*She stops short as she sees all the patients sitting, pencils in hand, looking blank*) Oh, how stupid can they be? (*She storms across in exasperation to each patient and points to the forms*) Name, number——
Jim (*passing close to the patients*) Next of kin.
Crisp (*furious at his flippancy*) Mr Pill!
Jim Keep your 'air on, Crispy. (*He moves to exit*)

Fred Bunch, a visitor, enters again from L clutching a bunch of daffodils. He bumps into Jim

Fred Excuse me, I'm making enquiries——
Jim Ask Cheese and Onion over there.

He indicates Miss Crisp and exits to help with sheets

Fred Excuse me could you help me. I'm making a routine check on——
Crisp Next door!
Fred Thank you very much.

Fred exits R

Nurse Bright enters from L

Crisp Good-morning Nurse Bright.
Bright Morning Crispy . . . er Miss Crisp. Lovely day.
Crisp (*acidly*) Lovely. (*She goes to the switchboard desk to finish admin. work*)
Bright (*spotting Jim, off*) Oh Jim, you're an angel.

Jim enters with two counterpanes

Jim Of course.
Bright You couldn't help me make up these beds for the new admissions could you?
Jim Yeah, course I can.
Bright You're smashing.

She gives Jim a playful kiss and Jim pretends to faint on the bed

Crisp (*looking up from her work and calling to the patients*) Form-fillers!

The patients all look up in unison

Finished?

The patients hold up their forms in unison

Fine!

Pleased, the patients clap themselves and accidentally drop their forms and scramble for them on the floor

Fools!

Matron sweeps in followed by Lint. She spots Bright and Jim

Matron (*referring to sheets*) Fold!
Lint Firmly! (*He speaks through his nose, sycophantically*)
Matron (*turning to him*) Lint! List!

Lint hands her the clipboard he is carrying. She looks at it, checking off patients. She pulls a biro from Lint's top pocket. He screams as if it's a part of his body. Lint then moves to the cubicle

Kipper case?

The patients all hold up their overnight bags in unison. Irritated, Matron signals for them to be put down

Not zipper case! Kipper case!
Kipper I'm ger kicker cake. (*That's how it comes out*)
Matron Casualty! (*She points to the cubicle*)

Lint draws back the curtains

Kipper Kank oo gery gutch. (*He walks into the cubicle*)

Lint pulls the curtains back over the entrance

Matron (*shouting to Kipper inside*) Shirt off!
Lint Trousers down! (*He peers in voyeuristically*)
Matron (*spotting him*) Lint!
Lint (*caught in the act*) Sorry, Matron. (*He is creepy and oily. He gooses Bright*)

Bright screams and jumps

Matron Lint!
Lint Coming Matron.

Lint and Matron exit

Crisp (*to the remaining two patients*) Pass your papers please.

They cross to Crisp, still clutching their overnight bags and hand her their papers which she stamps firmly

Perfect! (*She rubber stamps it*)

George and Doris jump in the air

Processed! (*She rubber stamps again*)

George and Doris jump again

Now Nurse Bright and the orderly will see you to your beds.
Bright Mrs Bucket? Is that right? (*She moves across to Mrs Bucket and takes her hand*)
Doris Bucket. That's right. (*She nods and smiles*)
Bright This way please. (*She moves towards the bed*)
Jim George Flower? (*He takes his hand*)
George That's me.
Jim Right, in you hop petal! (*Indicating the bed*)

Two screens are drawn round the beds. There is music. During the ensuing action Doris and George disrobe. Male clothing is draped over the screen on Doris's side and female clothing over the screen on George's side. The clothing is of course pre-set in the overnight bags. The clothes they are wearing are put into the bedside cabinets. Bright and Jim throw the clothes over while the patients undress. The audience should think that the patients are being undressed by Bright and Jim. There is some ad-lib dialogue behind the screens which Crisp should react to, but not so as to disturb the visual action out front

> *Fred Bunch enters, looking lost. A couple of the daffodils are broken. He is still looking for something. He moves to the cubicle to reveal . . .*

Kenneth Kipper in underpants, flat cap, string vest, boots and socks. He holds up his clothes in front of himself in embarrassment, emitting a scream

Kipper Aaagh!
Fred I say I'm most awfully sorry.
Kipper Gat's gall gite. (That's all right.)
Fred I wonder if you could possibly direct me to——
Crisp (*not looking up*) Ward Twelve! Surgical Appliances!
Fred Thank you so much, Ward Twelve. (*He replaces the cubicle curtain*) Ward Twelve . . . yes . . . now what's this?

He sees the screen round Doris's bed and, being curious sticks his head round the screen. Doris screams and when Fred jumps back he has a bra hanging from his mouth

Crisp (*seeing him*) What on earth are you doing?
Fred (*taking the bra out of his mouth*) Er, so sorry . . . I was looking for Ward Twelve to make enquiries about——

Doris grabs back the bra and Fred screams

Crisp That way. (*She points off*)
Fred That way. Yes of course, how silly of me. Ward Twelve . . . this way. (*He can't resist just one more look*)

Doris screams again and when his head reappears he has a pair of knickers in his mouth

Crisp Really!

Doris grabs them. Fred screams

Fred This way . . . right.

> *Fred exits*

During the whole piece of business we only see Doris's arm. Suddenly the switchboard buzzer sounds

Crisp Hello, St Sennapod's Hospital. Reception. Miss Crisp speaking, which department do you require? . . . (*Suddenly, her voice changes, gushingly*) Oh it's you, Dr Boldly. (*Pause*) Yes, Dr Boldly. (*Longer pause*) If you insist . . . Stephen. . . . You're coming up directly. Yes, of course, I'll tell (*acidly*) Nurse Bright. . . . Mr Lint would like the patients' folders. . . . Of course, Stephen . . . immediately.

Bright and Jim have now removed the screens to reveal Doris with foot and bucket on the pulley hoist. George is sitting up in bed. On the table trolley in front of him is a garden box containing plantpots, flowers, packets of seeds and a little trowel. He is busy potting plants. He waters them from the can on his head. The flower box was pre-set under the bed

> Mr Pill. (*She gets up and moves down the ward*) Mr Lint would like these files immediately. Please see that they are safely delivered to the main administration block.

Jim (*singing to the "Oliver" tune "I'd do Anything"*) "I'll do anything, for you 'salt and vinegar'. Anything."
Crisp Mr Pill!!
Jim Your word is my command! (*He starts to exit and then calls over his shoulder*) Crispy!

> *Jim exits with the files*

Crisp Nurse Bright. (*She spots Bright smirking*)
Bright (*forgetting*) Yes Crispy . . . er Miss Crisp. (*She is holding the pulley rope on Doris's leg*)
Crisp Dr Boldly . . .
Bright Dr Boldly! (*She pulls down on the pulley rope and Doris's foot flies up*)

Doris screams in agony

Crisp Yes. Dr Boldly, or (*pause*) "Stephen", as he prefers to be called by his closer colleagues, is on his way to examine the new admissions . . . or what's left of them.

The buzzer sounds and Crisp crosses to answer it

> Hello. St Sennapod's. May I help you? . . . Oh yes, Matron, I will be with you directly. (*She starts to go, then stops and addresses the audience*) Indispensable! (*She turns and walks straight into the path of . . .*)

. . . Boldly, as he enters R. *He has a pipe in his mouth*

Oh, Dr Boldly.

As he advances she walks backwards into the switchboard which buzzes as her bottom bumps against it. They both jump with a nervous "oops". She flutters nervously

Excuse me, Doctor, I have a Meetron with mating . . . er a meeting with Matron.

She exits R

Boldly Of course.

He turns—there is a moment when he sees Susan Bright, we hear music like the theme from "Love Story". They stare at each other. Doris is also transfixed. Boldly clicks his fingers and the Lights suddenly dim to a romantic pink. George can't see his plants and clicks his fingers and the Lights come back to normal. Boldly clicks, they are pink again. George looks up and is transfixed like Doris. Romantic music swells, and Boldly and Bright move to each other in slow motion until Boldly is one side of Doris's bed and Bright is the other side of George's bed. Boldly and Bright never take their eyes off each other throughout the following sequence

Nurse Bright.
Bright Dr Boldly.
Doris Mrs Bucket. (*She offers her hand to shake*)
George Mr Flower. (*He offers his hand to shake*)
Boldly How do you do. (*He takes Doris's hand and shakes it but never takes his eyes off Bright*)
Bright How do you do. (*She likewise shakes with George*)
Boldly (*sensuously*) Sooosan!
Bright Steeeephen!
Doris (*offering her hand*) Doris.
George (*offering his hand*) George.
Boldly (*as before*) How do you do.
Bright (*as before*) How do you do.
Boldly (*eyes on Bright*) Oh Susan, do you know how much I have been yearning for you?
Doris (*to Bright*) Do you know how much he's been yearning for you?
Boldly Wanting you.
Doris Wanting you.
Boldly Needing you.
Doris Needing you.
Bright Yes I do.
George (*to Boldly*) Yes she does.
Boldly (*suddenly moving to the ends of the two beds*) Oh, darling, can you remember the first time we met?
Bright (*moving to join him*) How can I ever forget?

George and Doris quietly hum the chorus tune of the song "Tuesday Tonsils" beneath the ensuing dialogue, accompanied by romantically choreographed movements in bed

Boldly We were in the Christmas panto together.
Bright Gosh yes. St Sennapod's "Cinderella".
Boldly Of course, and in the first act, you took the important part of Prince Charming.
Bright And in the second act you made me put it back. What madcap fools we were, Dr Boldly!
Boldly So silly!
Both So much in love!
Boldly And then our first meeting in the operating theatre.
Bright It was a Tuesday.
Boldly A tonsilectomy.
Bright It was so hot.
Boldly Damned hot!
Bright I felt faint, fell forward and grabbed your——
Boldly Stethoscope.
Bright Our eyes met.
Boldly And we knew that it was more than just a——
Bright |
Boldly | (*together*) —frivolous infatuation.
Bright Of course, Stephen, it was the real thing.
Boldly It was you.
Bright Tuesday.
Boldly And the tonsils.

Song 2: Tuesday, Tonsils And You

Boldly (*singing*)	Tuesday tonsils
Bright	Brought me to you
Boldly	Tuesday tonsils
Bright	True love for two
Boldly	Tuesday tonsils
Bright	Yes darling it's true
	Tuesday brought tonsils and you.

Boldly whirls away from the bed

Boldly	Who would have thought
	That two little warts
	Could bring paradise
Bright	That my heart would go zip
	When those two little snips
	Brought me to your side
Boldly	If tonsils could think
Bright	They'd be tickled pink
	Knowing they'd brought us so close
	Those two dinky danglers
	Like young Cupid's anglers
	Brought Tuesday, the tonsils and you.

George and Doris join in the last chorus. During this final chorus, Nurse Bright produces larger than life prop tonsils (fleshy coloured sleeves containing a large marble each)

All	Tuesday tonsils
	Brought me to you
	Tuesday tonsils
	True love for two
	Tuesday tonsils
	Yes darling it's true
	Tuesday brought tonsils and you.

Jim enters on the last line, carrying a surgical bowl

As he does so, Boldly mimics snipping each strand and they land with a loud clonk in Jim's bowl

Jim Thank you very much. (*He continues on and pulls back the cubicle curtain*)

Kipper is revealed painting and decorating the interior of the cubicle. Jim hands the bowl to Kipper

Kipper Kank ooo.

Boldly
Bright } (*together*) Jim!

Jim I came to warn you. Matron's on the warpath. Full warpaint and coming this way.

Boldly
Bright } (*together*) Oh no!

We hear a cod Indian war whoop off-stage as Matron, Crisp and Lint enter. Lint is actually making a war-cry sound until Matron smacks his face

Matron What is happening, Mr Pill?
Jim Sorry, Matron, I was just seeing to the Kipper in Casualty.

We hear the sound of water cascading into a container. It sounds like Kipper having a pee. Jim pulls back the curtain and we see Kenneth Kipper pouring water from a kettle into a teapot. They breathe a sigh of relief—more effective to have the kettle held a good distance from the teapot

Matron That's quite enough thank you, Pill.

Jim shuts the curtains

Now, I wish to speak to the entire staff on a matter of extreme importance.

Doris and George immediately lean forward, eager to hear gossip

(*Turning and looking at them*) PRIVATE importance!

They lean back and put on radio headphones. Lint has meanwhile moved to Doris's bed and after lifting her bed sheets is surreptitiously peering under the sheets

(*Spotting him*) Lint! What are you doing?!
Lint Just checking, Matron. Sorry, Matron.
Matron I think you had better join us, Mr Lint.
Lint Yes, Matron.
Matron Proceed please to the admin. desk where I shall require you to listen very carefully to what I have to say.
Boldly All very mysterious, Matron.

They move across to the low table as a complete group in unison, some sit, others stand in a group around the table

Matron I think that you had better prepare yourselves for a shock.
All Aaaaagh!
Matron There has been a catastrophe.
All No!
Crisp Not in administration I hope?
Bright Not in the nursing quarters?
Boldly Not in the operating theatre?
Jim Not in the linen cupboard?
Matron No. Worse, far worse.
Lint (*about to spill the beans*) The most celebrated surgeon that——
Matron (*interrupting*) Lint!
Lint Sorry, Matron.
Matron As I was about to explain . . . the most celebrated surgeon St Sennapod's has ever seen—(*she sprays them with sibilant spittle, Lint directly in the line of spray*)—I refer of course to——
Lint (*wiping his face*) Sir Barnaby Booth-Barrington!
Matron (*glaring at him for stealing her thunder*) Indeed. Sir Barnaby Booth-Barrington has unaccountably and quite inexplicably disappeared whilst en route for his annual vacation.
Lint To the Virgin Islands.
Matron Don't be filthy, Lint!
Lint No, Matron.
Boldly Good Lord, this is serious, (*he pulls out a pipe and jams it in mouth*) damned serious. You realize what this means?
Jim No.

The rest of the cast slowly enter for a song

Bright It means . . . patients unattended.
Lint Schedules upended.
Crisp Files to be amended.
Doris
       } (*together, looking happy and hopeful*) Operations suspended?
George
All (*turning to the patients*) Quiet!
Matron Rest assured, our first concern will be for the welfare of our patients——
Lint And St Sennapod's.
Matron Quite. Mr Lint and I will do our utmost to find a temporary replacement for Sir Barnaby.
Crisp But Sir Barnaby is irreplaceable.

The Company starts to assemble

Boldly Unique.
Jim Best in the business.

Song 3: Anthem to Sir Barnaby

The Company form a patriotic group

All
                                               With his great skill he cures us
                                               Of every known disease
                                               He snips and snaps and stitches
                                               Till all our pains are eased
                                               He has a shiny scalpel

All produce knives

                                             He has his trusty blade

All produce huge tools of some kind

> And with a knit one, purl one
> He sees our lives are saved

Sir Barnaby enters in a spot. He is wearing a swimsuit, flippers and snorkel and has a large hypodermic. He moves in slow motion then holds a pose like a statue

> All the staff around us
> Raise stethoscopes on high
> And praise his name
> Yes praise his name
> Sir B B Barrington

He squirts the hypo and sprays the front row of the audience. It should be a huge, long stream. Sir Barnaby exits

The children scream and the Lights go back to normal

Jim Cor! I feel better after that.

Matron Of course, but it still leaves us with a problem. Who can possibly take Sir Barnaby's place in the operating theatre?

Jim Well our assistants were very helpful earlier on when we had problems with the emergency patients.

Crisp Yes indeed. Maybe they could suggest someone who might have the skill and courage to take Sir Barnaby's place.

Cuddle Can you think of anybody that brave?

Pause

Bright Someone strong and handsome!

Pause

Jim Who smokes a pipe.

The children may immediately if not indirectly suggest Stephen Boldly. He is both surprised and embarrassed with the honour but strikes a noble pose, pipe in hand

Matron Dr Boldly?

All nurses rush to his side and freeze. He turns and looks at them

   They scream and exit

Cuddle Of course. Why didn't we think of Dr Boldly. Thank you so much.

Matron Very well. Dr Boldly, you will be totally responsible for ALL major surgery.

Boldly Is there any choice?

Lint Yes. Take it or leave it.

Boldly I'll do it.

Bright (*clutching his left arm*) Oh doctor!

Crisp (*clutching his right arm*) Oh Stephen!

Jim You must be mad!

Matron Pardon, Mr Pill.

Jim Er . . . that can't be bad.

   They are interrupted by a loud tapping on the rear window of the ward. It is Fred Bunch, now holding a very bedraggled bunch of daffodils, a bandage wound around his head as well as fingers

They all turn to look at him. He mouths the words but we can't hear him

Fred Which way?

All What?

Fred (*mouthing*) Which way?

All Where?

Fred The X-ray department.

Matron The X-ray department.

Fred Yes.

All (*pointing off* L) That way.

Fred Thank you.

   Fred exits

Matron (*clapping her hands*) Back to business. Lint. Time!

Lint Er . . . ten thirty-two precisely.

Matron Miss Crisp, how many "ops" scheduled for today?

Crisp (*consulting the clipboard*) Errr . . . just the one, Matron. (*She hands the board to Boldly*)

Boldly (*putting on his glasses*) My God ... it's a tummyectomy.

Stifled screams

　With cardionodular complications.

Loud shriek

Lint Nasty.
Jim
　　　　(*together*) Tricky.
Cuddle
Boldly Damned tricky.
Bright You can do it, Dr Boldly. Remember the tonsils.
Boldly How could I ever forget ... Susan.
Crisp (*sensing competition*) Will you need any extra help in the theatre, Stephen?
Boldly Yes, we're going to need all the damned help we can damn well get.
Crisp (*in a deep voice*) Then I'm your man.
Jim That's true. I'll bring the patient in. (*He starts to exit*)
Crisp I'll clear the theatre out. (*She starts to exit*)
Bright I'll wash the patient down.
Cuddle I'll dry him. (*She starts to exit*)
Boldly I'll scrub up. (*He starts to exit*)
Lint I'll just stick my hand right up and—(*Putting on rubber gloves and thinking of something particularly vulgar*)
Matron No you will not, Mr Lint! Efficiency is all we need. Bright, check the emergency patient.
Bright Immediately, Matron.

　All except Bright, Matron and Lint exit

Bright checks on Kipper, drawing back the curtain. It reveals Kipper making himself at home. He has been waiting so long to be seen that he has now decorated his little "house" and is sitting back pouring tea from the teapot and eating a meal. He offers her a cup of tea

Kipper (*holding out a cup*) Gice gucka gee?
Bright Not just now, Mr Kipper. I'll be back in a minute.

　Bright closes the curtains and exits

Kipper Gokey goke. (Okey doke.)

Lint has moved silently towards Doris's bed and, as Doris and George seem to be fast asleep, he is about to pinch some of Doris's grapes when Matron spots him

Matron Lint!
Lint Sorry, Matron, just checking the patient's grapes ... er ... (*stroking the curtain on the rear window*) ... drapes. (*But he still has the bunch in his other hand*)
Matron They don't need checking, but Dr Boldly will need Sir Barnaby's surgical notes for the tummyectomy. Give me a hand to look for them.
Lint Certainly, Matron. (*He waves his hand in agreement and, in so doing, reveals the bunch of grapes*) Oops, sorry, Matron! (*He places the grapes back on the plate*)
Matron Look in the filing cabinet.
Lint Certainly, Matron. (*He pops the grapes back into his coat pocket*)
Matron And get rid of those grapes.
Lint Of course, Matron. (*He starts to eat them greedily, noisily*)

The children will react

Matron Now!

Lint chucks them into the auditorium

　Bright enters with a trolley

Bright I found this trolley in the corridor, Matron. It must be the patient for surgery.
Matron (*impatiently*) All right, all right, Nurse Bright. Just leave the trolley there.

　Bright exits, leaving the trolley covered with a large sheet

Lint I've found the notes, Matron. (*He hands her a file*)
Matron Thank you, Lint, I just hope Dr Boldly is up to this.
Lint He's up to most things, Matron.
Matron Uncalled for, Lint.
Lint Just a jokey, Matron.

Matron Jokey? This is no time for jokeys. (*She smacks him round the face*)

They exit

The sheet-covered trolley remains C *as the Lights fade slightly and we hear sinister surgical music. Flower and Bucket snooze. Tootski and Scalpel are hidden from view under the sheet. They are lying head to foot*

Tootski Dr Scalpel?
Scalpel (*also whispering from the other end of the trolley*) Tootski?
Tootski (*whispering*) Do-you-think-the-coast-is-clear?
Scalpel I don't know. Haff a schniff around.

Tootski shoots out a huge deformed foot, wiggles it about making sniffing noises

Tootski Feels all right, smells all right. Yes. I don't think we have been spotted.
Scalpel (*slowly appearing at the other end of the trolley*) Zis is excellent. (*He turns and spots Tootski's foot*) Aaagh! Put zat away, you fool.

Tootski's foot shoots back

It's ze most hideous zing I haf ever seen in my life.

Tootski's face appears at the other end of the trolley

Well, almost the most hideous zing I haf ever seen in my life.
Tootski What a brilliant plan, master.
Scalpel Quite brilliant.
Tootski Sneaking secretly into St Sennapod's.
Scalpel Quite schneaky.
Tootski Infiltrating its inner recesses.
Scalpel Don't be disgustink!
Tootski Forgive me. What do we do next, master? Do we join in Dr Boldly's operation and surreptitiously snaffle as many of the patients' bits and pieces as we can?
Scalpel Are you off your trolley?
Tootski Not yet, master, I'm descending now. (*She starts to get down*)
Scalpel No, lunatic! Are you out of your tiny mind!
Tootski I've said something stupid?
Scalpel You certainly haff. Don't you realize zis part of ze plan is purely exploratory. (*Getting down off the trolley*)
Tootski Exploratory?
Scalpel Of course, a chance to familiarize ourselves viz ze layout of St Schennapod's before we strike . . . tonight.
Tootski We'll be sneaking in the hospitals, searching high and low?
Scalpel We'll be stealing all the spare parts and nobody will know. Tootski.
Tootski Master?
Scalpel I feel a song coming on.
Tootski Marvellous!

Song 4: Nickin' Bits in the Night

Scalpel \
Tootski /

We'll be sneaking in the hospitals
Searching high and low
We'll be stealing all the spare parts
And nobody will know
Any old leg or foot or toe
To us is pure delight
So hold on to everything nice and tight
We're nickin' bits in the night

We'll be using all our trickery
Dirty deeds to do
We'll be creeping in your bedroom
And cutting off lumps of you
Any old leg or foot or toe
To us is pure delight
So hold on to everything nice and tight
We're nickin' bits in the night

We are masters of the universe
Heartless, cold as ice
And when we've got the rumps and stumps
You'll have to pay our price

Any old leg or foot or toe
To us is pure delight
So hold on to everything nice and tight
We're nickin' bits in the
Cuttin' bits off yer
Nickin' bits in the night

They cackle, etc.

Scalpel I feel so much better after a song, Tootski.
Tootski Refreshed, master.
Scalpel Rejuvenated! Now back to business.
Tootski The final plan.
Scalpel Ze final plan as you say, Tootski. Zis ward seems ze perfect place to hide all ze bits ve nick in ze night.
Tootski The night-nicked bits.
Scalpel Yes. Ve vill finish our fiendish work at St Hilary's hospital down ze road and then present ourselves to Miss Crust . . .
Tootski (*correcting him*) Crisp.
Scalpel Crusp, yes, as Sir Barnaby's new replacement.
Tootski (*sarcastically*) Dear Sir Barnaby.
Scalpel What a pity he had to disappear like that.
Tootski Absolutely.

They snigger

Scalpel But there are some loose ends to tie up.
Tootski (*looking down at her foot*) Are there?
Scalpel Yes. Ve must find some schtupid visitor to take our place on the operation trolley.

Fred Bunch enters holding daffodils. He is clearly delirious and confused

Fred (*muttering*) Make enquiries . . . Ward Twelve . . . turn left . . . turn right . . . surgical appliances . . . must make routine enquiries . . . X-ray department . . . this way.
Scalpel Excuse me, are you a visitor?
Fred I am (*nearly in a trance*) making enquiries.
Tootski Are you slightly stupid?
Fred Yes . . . I am making enquiries.
Scalpel Pefect. (*To Tootski*) Anaesthetic, Tootski!

Tootski hits him over the head with an enormous hammer secreted in his arm sling. There is a loud "pop" and Fred conveniently collapses on to the trolley

Scalpel Made to measure.
Tootski Perfect fit.

They pull the sheet over him. The sheet has a hole in it through which the daffodils stick up. We hear noises off-stage of Matron, Lint and Jim returning

Scalpel Quickly, zey are returning. Now, back to St Hilary's to pick up ze kneecaps and zen "Operation Sennapod's"!

They cackle and start to exit—half-way across Scalpel stops and turns to Tootski

Pick your feet up!
Tootski Sorry, master.

They exit

Matron, Lint and Jim enter. They are all in operating theatre gear with masks round their necks

Matron (*as she enters*) Just concentrate please on keeping this hospital clean and tidy and . . . (*she spots the trolley*) . . . what's that trolley doing there, Lint?
Lint (*turning to Jim*) What's that trolley doing there, Pill? Just concentrate please on keeping this hospital clean and tidy.
Jim All right, all right. Don't get your truss in a twist, Linty. I'll get the patient ready for his "op".

He exits, wheeling the trolley off

Lint Tell me, Matron, what sort of a chance does that patient stand in the hands of Dr Boldly?

He sidles across to Matron who is engrossed in reading the notes

Matron Well, I wouldn't advise him to start reading any serials.

They both laugh

Lint Who's doing jokeys now, Matron?

She slaps his face

Sorry, Matron.

Bright enters with a huge hypodermic

Bright Shall I give the patient his anaesthetic, Matron?
Matron Yes, yes. How would this hospital run without me?
Lint Very well.

Matron looks at Lint. There is a moment, he offers his cheek submissively and she slaps his face again

Not very well, Matron, not very well at all.

Lint and Matron remain where they are

Matron Dr Boldly, we-are-ready-for-you.

The Lights dim down and we hear very quietly the ominous soundtrack music of a hospital B-movie. Jim enters pushing the trolley and behind is a procession. The Company are in operating gear with masks round their mouths. When they are in position Dr Boldly is in the centre behind the trolley with Nurse Bright by his side. There is a bright downward spot on the trolley and Fred Bunch. We hear heavy breathing

Flower and Bucket sit up in bed—they have masks on too. We hear heartbeats accompanied by all the sounds of electrical paraphernalia that one associates with large surgical operations. Suddenly Boldly raises his hands and there is silence

Boldly Gloves!

Jim helps him on with a household rubber glove on his right arm and then repeats with the left. The Company copy his moves. When the gloves are on he twiddles his finger, the Company do the same until Boldly catches them at it

Hypodermic!

Bright hands him the huge hypo which he rams into Fred

All Ugh!

As Boldly pushes down the plunger, there are more gurgling noises (made by the Company) as liquid supposedly pours in. He pulls it out and the Company all make popping sounds with their fingers in their mouths

All Pop!

Boldly places his hands around the bunch of flowers Fred is holding. He slowly unscrews the flowers as the Company make unscrewing noise, a pop again as the flowers are extracted. He gives them to Miss Crisp. She smells them and is obviously flattered. Boldly pulls down his mask and sings. The song should be heavily choreographed with unison movements involving the whole company, and presented in the style of a big number like "I Did It My Way"

Song 5: I've Left My Gloves In

Boldly

And now the time is come
And so I'll face my greatest challenge
Nurse Bright you're by my side
I'll do my best to use my talents
I worked so hard at nights
I studied each and every problem
But more
Much more than this, I stitched 'em neatly
Yes there'd be times, I knew there would
When I'd snip off more than I should

He snips with scissors

But through it all when there were doubts
I took the plunge cut big lumps out

He produces garden shears

I faced it all and I stood tall
And stitched 'em neatly

The Lights dim and concentrate on Boldly as Bright passes him a scalpel and pieces of surgical equipment, during the next verse

> So now I'll start the op
> And so I'll face this tricky puncture
> Nurse Bright pass me the knife

She does

> I'll do my best at this tight juncture
> I've found the cause of pain (*He peers inside*)
> I'm stitching each and every vein up
> But more
> Much more than this, I think I've cured him!

All Hurrah!

They pull down their masks and sing with increasing fervour as Boldly is removing his gloves unseen by the audience

> (*singing*)   Yes there'd be times, he knew there would
> When he'd snip off more than he should
> But through it all, when there was doubt
> He took the plunge, cut big lumps out
> He faced it all and he stood tall . . .

A long pause

Boldly (*in horror*)   . . . but left my gloves in!

Mad music as they start to rummage around and pull out all sorts of silly things, old kettles, sausages, intestines, teddy bears etc. and finally he finds the gloves and holds them up. The Lights come up

All He did it his way!

Streamers are thrown, party poppers, shrieks and everyone congratulates each other, especially Boldly. They put on paper party hats

Matron (*as the operation reaches its triumphant conclusion*) Congratulations, Dr Boldly.
Jim Yeah, well done mate. You sewed him up a treat. A quick round of applause I think.

They respond

Crisp Dear Sir Barnaby would have been proud of you.
Bright Oh Ste—— Dr Boldly, you were wonderful.
Boldly Well I must admit it was tricky at times, damned tricky but I think we made it in time. (*He looks at his wrist-watch but it has disappeared*) Oh gosh I've lost my watch.
Matron All right, Dr Boldly, no time for post mortems now.
Jim That'll come later!
Matron I beg your pardon, Mr Pill?
Jim (*fumbling with his diary*) I said "I'll just check the data".
Matron Please take this patient down to the recovery room.
Jim Right you are.

> *He turns to wheel patient off on the trolley*

Meanwhile Lint is peering beneath the sheet

Matron Lint!
Lint Er, might I have a word, Matron? I think we've operated on the wrong person. It's a mistake.
Matron Mistake? The only mistake here is you, Mr Lint. Remove your hand from the patient immediately. You and Dr Boldly will follow me to my office where we shall confer about the permanent replacement for Sir Barnaby.
Lint But Matron, it's that stranger that was making enquiries——
Matron Immediately, Mr Lint!
Lint Very well, Matron. (*He turns with resignation and begins to follow Matron off*)

> *Jim wheels the trolley off*

Throughout the above dialogue, Boldly and Bright have been staring adoringly into each other's eyes, oblivious to the rest of the world

Matron Dr Boldly!
Boldly Yes, Angelface? Er . . . Certainly, Matron. Immediately, Matron.

He exits after Matron and Lint

Crisp is taking off her gown when the switchboard buzzer sounds

Crisp Oh, a woman's work is never done! Hello, St Sennapod's, may I help you? . . . Yes, certainly, I'll tell her now. (*She puts down the phone*) Nurse Bright!

Bright is staring off into space at the receding figure of Boldly

Nurse Bright!
Bright Yes, darling. I was just——
Crisp I am fully aware of what you were "just" doing, Nurse Bright. Please pull yourself together. Mr Flower and Mrs Bucket should have been at Physiotherapy five minutes ago.
Bright Oh gosh, so sorry, I'll see to it now. (*She goes to Bucket and Flower to wake them up*) Come along, Mrs Bucket. Up you get, Mr Flower. We're off to Physio.
George I was just getting my bedding plants down.
Doris And very nice they look too, Mr Flower.
George Thank you very much. You know, my real friends call me George.
Doris George? That's a lovely name. Well I shall call you George from now on then, Mr Flower.
George I shall like that . . . Doris.
Doris Ooh! You're a fast worker, Mr Flower.
George George.
Doris George.
George You don't look very well, Doris. Everything all right is it?
Doris No, it's this bucket, George, it's making me feel really poorly.
George Yes—you do look a little pale. Oops!

They chuckle at the pun as they exit with Nurse Bright

Crisp It's a good job somebody in this hospital knows what they're doing.

A loud groan is heard from the cubicle

Kipper (*from behind the curtain*) I can't get ITV. The gicture's gone all gunny. (The picture's gone all funny.)

Crisp moves over to the cubicle, pulls aside the curtain. Kipper is fiddling with the TV. The standard lamp is on, with an easy chair and pictures on the wall

Crisp Don't be impatient, Mr Kipper, somebody will see to you in a moment. (*She closes the curtains*) I don't know what the world is coming to. In my day patients were patient.

Jim pushes in

Jim Miss Crisp—can you come. It's the bloke who was operated on. He says there's a funny bleeping noise coming from his tummy every fifteen minutes.
Crisp Oh for heaven's sake, is this another Boldly boob?

She exits with Jim

Cuddle enters L from the lift, calling

Cuddle Miss Crisp! There's a strange man and his assistant just arrived and . . . (*she can't see her*) . . . Miss Crisp? (*To the audience*) Have you seen Miss Crisp? . . . She went where? . . . Out there? Thank you. (*She is stopped by Kipper's voice*)
Kipper (*from the cubicle*) The gicture's all guzzy. I gight giss GeastGenders! (The picture's all muzzy. I might miss EastEnders!)
Cuddle Looks like Mr Kipper needs help. I think he's nice, don't you? (*She pulls back the curtains*) Can I help you at all, Mr Kipper?

They look at each other then out front. It's clearly love at first sight. Kipper pulls out a huge cardboard heart and places it between them, there is a bell-like ding, their eyelids flutter and Kipper pulls Cuddle into the cubicle. She emits a yelp of delight as the curtains close

Miss Crisp enters

Crisp Did I hear somebody calling me? (*To the audience*) Who was it? Nurse Cuddle? Well, where is she? . . . In the cubicle helping Mr Kipper. Well, thank you very much for your help. (*She goes to the cubicle*) Are you all right in there?
Kipper (*lecherously, from the cubicle*) Yeg gank oo gery gutch! (Yes thank you very much!)
Crisp Nurse Cuddle.
Cuddle (*from the cubicle*) Mmmm! Everything's lovely thank you, Miss Crisp.

Cuddle and Kipper both giggle

Crisp Really! Well, back to work. I hope that nothing else will disturb the day! (*She opens a large box to get out a pen*)

Tootski (*off, from the lift, screaming*) Aaaagh! My foot!!

The door opens and Tootski and Scalpel emerge. Tootski limps and Scalpel is carrying a large suitcase

Scalpel Good-afternoon. Allow me to introduce myself. My name is DR SCALPEL! (*He whips out a huge carving knife*)

As Scalpel delivers this last line, Boldly, Bright, Matron, Lint and Pill enter from different entrances

The cubicle curtain flashes back and they all freeze with a scream after the word "SCALPEL" when he whips out the carving knife. Crisp shuts the lid of her box in fear on to her fingers and screams. Scalpel drops the suitcase on to Tootski's foot. Tootski grabs the foot and screams. Everybody freezes. Black-out. "Nickin' Bits in the Night" is played as the stage clears and the House Lights come up

CURTAIN

ACT II

The act opens with a re-enactment of the end of Act I except that the stage does not clear

Scalpel Good-afternoon, allow me to introduce myself. My name is Dr Scalpel.

Business with box and suitcase as at the end of Act I

Crisp (*jumping up*) What is going on here! Really, it may have escaped your attention but this is a hospital not a repository for left luggage. Remove that bag and the rest of you get about your business.
All Yes, Miss Crisp.

They exit

Crisp Now your card please.

There is a sequence of funny business when the trio pass the card, suitcase and Scalpel's knife between them until eventually Crisp ends up with the card

Scalpel Allow me to introduce myself, dear madame. Ze name is Scalpel, Dr Scalpel, MD, Dip. Sheep, Maniac, SRN.
Crisp SRN?
Scalpel Yes. State Registered Nutcase.

He and Tootski have hysterics

Crisp (*impressed*) I see. How do you do, Dr Scalpel.
Scalpel (*indicating Tootski*) And zis is my assistant . . .
Tootski Personal scientific assistant.
Scalpel (*glaring at Tootski*) Quite, my personal scientific assistant, Tootski.
Crisp (*coldly, with a nod in her direction*) How do you do.
Scalpel I am here as dear Sir Barnaby Barrington's replacement.
Tootski He's a very important person.
Scalpel (*under his breath*) Shut up!
Crisp I do apologize for the mistake, Dr Scalpel.
Scalpel Quite understandable, Miss er——
Crisp Crisp.
Scalpel Miss Crisp. Now, I zink zat, if you contact Matron, you vill find zat ve are expected.
Crisp Certainly, Dr Scalpel. (*She phones through on the switchboard*) Hello Matron, Miss Crisp speaking . . . *etc.*

During the above Scalpel pulls Tootski downstage and the following whispered conversation unheard by Crisp ensues

Scalpel Vell ve are here, no zanks to you!
Tootski I tell you she is suspicious already.
Scalpel Nonsense, ze plan is foolproof. (*He looks at Tootski*) It has to be wiz you around. Just don't put your foot in it!
Tootski (*shouting*) Don't mention my foot!
Scalpel (*hand over her mouth*) Ssh, are you trying to attract attention? Just act normally, if zat is possible. (*He turns and smiles at Crisp*)
Crisp (*putting the phone down*) Matron says that if you and your assistant——
Tootski Personal scientific assistant!
Crisp Quite, if you would like to make yourselves at home in the reception area—(*she indicates the area*)—she will be along to welcome you personally.
Scalpel Zank you, Miss Crisp. Tootski, ze case.

Tootski sighs, and picking up the case, moves towards the reception area

Crisp Well, Dr Scalpel, if there's nothing else, I'll leave you to settle in.
Scalpel No, no, no, ve vill be fine, Miss Crisp, zank you so much. (*He offers his hand to shake—he has a vice-like grip*)
Crisp Oh the pleasure's all mine, Dr Scalpel.

She exits with crooked hand

Scalpel moves to the office area where Tootski has left the case

Scalpel Vat did I tell you? No problems.
Tootski I hope you are right.
Scalpel Of course I am. Now check zat ze coast is clear and zen help me unpack zis case before that busybody Matron arrives.

They both freeze when they hear voices from the cubicle plus the sound of the "Wedding March". Tootski moves towards the cubicle and whips back the curtain to reveal . . .

Kipper and Nurse Cuddle being married by a Vicar (who enters and exits by the rear doorway in the cubicle). Cuddle has a veil and posy, Kipper is in a topper

Vicar Do you, Kenneth Kipper, take this woman Louise Cuddle to be your lawful wedded wife?
Kipper Guy goo. (I do.)
Vicar Then I pronounce you Mr and Mrs Kipper.

They hug

Tootski They're all bonkers here!
Vicar You may kiss the Kipper. (*He throws confetti over them and shakes hands*)
Scalpel Tootski! Heel! Close zose curtains and giff me ze key quickly!

Tootski does as she is told and returns

The Vicar exits from the cubicle

Tootski Ze key for what?
Scalpel Ze key for ze case, you fool.
Tootski (*opening a small trapdoor in her toecap and taking out a key on a string*) Here it is.

She waves it in front of Scalpel who momentarily becomes hypnotized

Scalpel (*pulling himself together*) Stop pussy-footing around and get ze case open . . .

The case is opened to reveal a variety of limbs, noses, hands, ears, etc.

Vot a collection, Tootski, ve haf done vell.
Tootski Very vell.
Scalpel But not well enough—ve are (*spitting*) schtill schort of schome schpecimens.
Tootski Schpray zat again.
Scalpel Let us check ze schpare parts. Hands?
Tootski Mmmm.
Scalpel Knees.
Tootski Mmm.
Scalpel Unt . . .
Tootski Boom—sa—daisy.

They start to dance

Scalpel Don't be schtupid, Tootski. Zis is a serious matter. Schtop acting ze fool and toe ze line.
Tootski Sorry, Dr S.
Scalpel How many hospitals have ve infiltrated now?
Tootski Six.
Scalpel Six successful surgical separations! You know vot zis means, don't you, Tootski.

They both laugh sardonically

Tootski (*stopping laughing*) No.
Scalpel It means zat already six major medical establishments vill pay any price for our spare parts.
Tootski Top prices for tootsie transplants!
Scalpel Yes it's a tremendous feat.

They both look down at Tootski's foot, then at each other, then out front

Tootski Don't be personal!
Scalpel Don't be sensitive. Ve are still many anatomical pieces short before ve can totally control ze vorld market. Ve still need . . .
Tootski Brains?
Scalpel (*looking knowingly at Tootski*) Yes.

Tootski Biceps?
Scalpel Yes.
Tootski Botties?
Scalpel If you insist.
Tootski And don't forget . . .
Scalpel Yes, Tootski, a new foot for yourself.
Tootski Then I can be normal.
Scalpel If you think that's possible. Now vere are ve going to conceal ze case?
Tootski In zat cupboard. (*She points to the cupboard in a corner of the set*)
Scalpel Excellent! (*He fits the case in with difficulty*) Made to measure.

> *They are interrupted by the arrival of Matron, Lint, Crisp and Boldly*

Crisp This way, Matron. I told them to make themselves comfortable in the reception area.
Matron Thank you, Miss Crisp, this is a medical matter. I will deal with it.
Crisp I know when I'm not wanted. If I am needed again you know where to find me . . . (*pointedly at Matron*) . . . Stephen. (*She flounces to the switchboard*)
Boldly (*embarrassed*) Oh quite . . . thank you, Miss Crisp.
Lint (*sneering*) Creep!
Boldly No, "Crisp".

> *Scalpel and Tootski come out to meet them*

Matron I'm so sorry that the senior staff were not here to meet you personally, Dr Scalpit.
Scalpel Scalpel.
Matron Pardon?
Scalpel Scalpel, ze name is Scalpel not Scalpit. Dr Scalpel and zis is my assistant . . .
Tootski Personal scientific assistant.
Scalpel (*wearily*) Personal scientific assistant, Tootski. And you are?
Matron So sorry. Clamp! Miss Clamp, Matron. Allow me to introduce Dr Stephen Boldly, who has been holding the fort since the unaccountable disappearance of Sir Barnaby.
Boldly (*extending his pipe towards Scalpel*) Pleased to meet you, sir.
Scalpel Ze pleasure is mine.
Boldly No no, the pleasure is all mine.
Scalpel Nonsense, I insist ze pleasure is totally mine.
Boldly Oh I don't know, I think the pleasure is——

> *They shake hands—there is a huge crunching sound*

Scalpel Don't argue wiz me!
Boldly (*high-pitched/hoarse*) Certainly not.
Matron Thank you, Dr Boldly. Miss Crisp (*she nods in her direction*) you've already met. These young people have been helping during the emergency. (*She smiles at the audience*)
Scalpel They look troublesome. (*He sneers at the audience*)
Matron Well I think that's everybody.
Lint (*dry cough*) Ahem.
Matron Oh I'm so sorry. How could I forget. Lint! Administration. (*The way she speaks indicates that she considers Lint a second-class citizen!*)
Lint Yes, Doctor, I keep a check on everything and everybody. (*He chuckles*) There's very little I miss. "Little lurking Lint" I was known as in my student days. Eh, Matron?
Matron Quite, Lint.
Lint You managed to arrive surprisingly quickly, Dr Scalpel. We had only just alerted the Emergency Doctor service.
Tootski Well St Hilary's is only just round the corner——
Scalpel (*interrupting*) Er . . . yes . . . we came "hot foot"——

> *He glances at Tootski's foot, same look, business as before by all*

—as soon as we were informed of your predicament.

> *Jim Pill and Nurse Bright burst in with George and Doris—either on a trolley or walking wounded, returned from physiotherapy, carrying the bucket and watering can*

Jim Watch out! Keep well back!
Bright Mind the door!
Jim Special delivery!
Doris I'm not a maternity case you know.

George (*with a dirty laugh*) Not yet you're not!

Doris You little tinker, Mr . . . George!

Bright Mr Flower!!

Matron Really, Nurse Bright, Mr Pill. This levity is quite uncalled for. What will Dr Scalpel and his assistant think of St Sennapod's? Please keep the patients under control.

Jim Sorry, Matron, they just got a bit over-excited.

George 'Cause we're cured.

Doris Sorted out!

Bright Yes, isn't it wonderful! Five minutes in physio with Mr Wrench and they're completely cured.

George De-canned! (*He holds up the watering can*)

Doris De-bucketed! (*She holds up bucket*)

Boldly Delightful!

Matron Well get those patients into bed. They obviously need a short period of convalescence. Dr Boldly, please check that there are no complications. Meanwhile, Dr Scalpel, maybe you and your assistant——

Tootski (*furious*) Personal scientific assistant!!

Matron —yes, would like to accompany Mr Lint and myself on a tour of the hospital. (*As they move off, she looks at Crisp*) Crisp! Coffee!

Lint Coffee! Crisp!

Crisp Hmm. Yes, Matron.

She exits, muttering words like "a domestic skivvy that's what I've become, never appreciated, only to be expected" etc.

Matron, Lint, Scalpel and Tootski exit the opposite way

The ensuing dialogue takes place as Doris and George are helped into bed by Bright and Boldly

Boldly Now, Mrs Bucket, sit on the edge of the bed. How do you feel?

Doris Me arms hurt, me neck hurts and me chest hurts.

Boldly (*banging her knee with a reflex hammer*) Now how do you feel?

Doris Me knee hurts too!

They all laugh

Jim Come along, Mrs Bucket, you heard what her ladyship said, let's get you tucked in and tucked up, you need a rest.

Doris Well I must admit, I could do with a rest, I've had fifteen kids and three husbands but that's nothing to the pain I felt when he wrenched my leg.

Bright Three husbands! Goodness, what on earth happened to them all?

Doris They all kicked the bucket, didn't they! I'm looking for number four.

Bright Ooh, there you are, Mr Flower, you're in with a chance if you're quick.

George Got to get me leeks in first, 'aven't I?

Jim I shouldn't take too long, Mr Flower! Where's the local paper, Nurse Bright?

Bright (*moving to the table*) Here it is, Jim.

Jim Right, let's see how the lads got on in Saturday's match.

Bright I'll just check the linen.

Jim settles down with the paper

Boldly I'll help you with the pillows, Nurse Bright.

Bright Oh Stephen . . .

They exit

The Lights dim in the reception area to leave the beds in a pool of light

George You awake, Doris?

Doris No . . . (*With a chuckle*) Yes, course I am.

George I think you're the funniest lady I've ever met.

Doris George Flower, that's the nicest thing anyone's ever said to me.

George When we get out of here I'm gonna take you down my allotment.

Doris Is that good?

George Never taken no lady down there afore.

Doris Then I shall be very proud to go, George.

George Good. Well that's settled then.

Doris What's settled?

Song 6: Come to My 'Lotment

George	I'll pick you a nosegay, a lovely bouquet
	Of flowers from my 'lotment, some fine summer's day
	A sweet little posy, especially for you
	Of poppies and pansies and cornflowers blue

Doris (*speaking*) Oh, Mr Flower.

George (*singing*)	And if you would like a fresh 'tater or two
	Just come to my 'lotment, there's plenty for you
	There's carrots and spinach for you my sweetheart
	And raspberries for making a raspberry tart

Doris (*speaking*) Could I help?
George (*speaking*) Course you could.

(*singing*)	Then I'll fill your bucket with beetroot and beans
	And fresh crispy lettuce and broc'li and greens
	There'll be turnips and green beans and marrows so fine ...

They pause and look at each other

Won't you come to my 'lotment—be my Valentine?

Doris (*speaking*) Course I will.
George (*speaking*) Luverly. 'Ave a goosegog. (*He passes her one*)
Doris (*speaking*) Ta!

They both dive under the covers. The Lights fade on them. The Lights come up on Jim at the table. Jim breaks the moment as ...

Bright enters carrying a pile of sheets. She places them on the locker top

Jim (*reading the local paper*) 'Ere you seen this, Nurse Bright?
Bright What's that?
Jim Look. In the paper. Front page news "Hospital Scandal of the Missing Bits".
Doris Ooh! I wonder what that Mr Lint's been up to now.
Jim No, it ain't St Sennapod's, it's St Hilary's. Listen to this. "Officials at St Hilary's Hospital are today refusing to comment on the spate of mysterious thefts at the hospital."
Bright Crikey!
Jim "It appears that patients' personal private parts have been pinched from their persons!"
Bright That's terrible, Jim.
Jim "Mrs Edna Entwhistle a patient at St Hilary's said 'One minute my nose was there, the next it had gone. I felt no pain, merely inconvenience. I blame the cuts in the NHS myself.'"
Bright Well what do the hospital managers say about it?
Jim "A hospital spokesman did admit that some patients seemed to have temporarily mislaid minor parts of their anatomy, adding that there was no cause for alarm because, in any large organization one had to expect a certain amount of petty pilfering."
Doris (*sitting up*) Petty pilfering! I hope no-one's going to start pilfering my personal parts.
George (*sitting up*) Nor mine neither.
Jim You hold on to all your bits, mate.
George I will, don't you worry. We're going down the 'lotment later.
Doris (*coyly*) George!
Bright I'm sure we're all quite safe here, particularly with Ste—— Dr Boldly around.
Jim Yeah, but you can't be too careful, not where your personal bits is concerned. (*He puts the paper in his pocket*)

Boldly enters

Boldly Right, let's cut the cackle and get down to the serious stuff. Checks have to be made. I will take Mr Flower's ... er ... um ... ah ...
Bright Pulse?
Boldly Exactly, Mr Flower's pulse, and er Susan, maybe you would be kind enough to take Mrs Bucket's er ... um ... ah ...
Bright Blood-pressure?
Boldly Precisely.

They get into position between the two beds, back to back

Jim I'll just pop these things in the office and then you can take them home as souvenirs. (*He indicates the bucket and watering can*)

Doris
George } (*together*) Thanks very much, dear. How thoughtful ... *etc.*

Jim Here we go. (*He picks up the bucket and watering can*) I'll take their files back to the office too, Doc.

Jim exits

Boldly Good idea, Jim. Damned good idea.

There is a moment when Bright and Boldly turn to face each other

Bright Oh Stephen, alone at last. (*Two puffs on the blood-pressure kit attached to Doris*)
Boldly Working together, hand in hand.

They hold hands. Boldly goes to take George's pulse but takes his leg instead. A balloon is attached to the blood-pressure kit. Bright puffs the b.p. kit, the puffs becoming more frequent and frenzied in keeping with the passion of the scene. Boldly lifts George's leg inch by inch

Bright Have you any idea how much I've missed you?
Boldly Not half as much as I've missed you.
Bright Really?
Boldly Truly? We must meet.
Bright When?
Boldly Tonight.
Bright Where?
Boldly Here.
Bright Here?
Boldly In the ward.
Bright Time?
Boldly Ten to ten.
Bright I'll be on tenterhooks till ten.
Boldly When?
Bright Ten to ten.
Boldly Till then.

Jim enters and spots the cupboard ajar

Jim Blimey, who left this open! I'm always tidying up after patients. (*He pulls Scalpel's case out of the cupboard*) Does anybody own this?

The case falls open and as the missing bits fall out, the following happens. Jim screams

Matron and Lint enter carrying a large pile of files which they drop, screaming

Crisp enters carrying a tray of coffee which she drops, with a scream

Kipper and Cuddle in night-clothes whip back the cubicle curtains and scream. Doris bursts the balloon on her blood-pressure kit. She and George scream

Blimey, it's full of missing bits!

All look at the bits, then at each other then out front then …

All Aaaaagh!

When they have recovered, Matron breaks the silence

Matron Mr Pill, where did you get that revolting receptacle!
Jim I ffffound it in the ccccupboard by the ttttable.

Lint moves across curiously

Matron What does it contain?
Lint Let me examine its contents. (*He holds up each limb in turn*) A Horrible Hand!
Boldly A Festering Foot!
Bright A Nobbly Nose!
Kipper A Fishy Finger!

He and Cuddle disappear back into the cubicle

Jim A Severed Scalp! (*He holds up a hairpiece*)
Crisp Bits of Bone! (*She shakes a tin that rattles*)
George
Doris } (*together*) Amputated Ear 'oles!!

All scream

Matron Silence! Where in the name of St Sennapod's have they come from?
Bright No idea.
Boldly Not a clue.
Lint Search me.
Matron No thank you, Lint!

They all look at Crisp

Crisp Don't look at me.
Boldly By George I've got it. I think I've got it.
Doris
George } (*singing in tempo, clicking castanets*) "The rain in Spain stays mainly on the plain."
All By George he's got it. I think he's got it.
Matron Stop it! Explain yourself, Dr Boldly. Get a grip on yourselves, you two.

George's and Doris's hands dive under the sheets

Boldly I've just remembered, Jim's paper. The headlines.
Lint Headlines? Jim's paper? What are you babbling about?
Bright Of course, Stephen. The bits.
Crisp Bits?
Bright Yes the missing bits.
Crisp (*looking at herself doubtfully*) Missing bits?
Boldly Patients' personal private parts pilfered from St Hilary's Hospital.
Matron Revolting!
Jim He's right you know. Where's my paper? (*He pulls it out*) Here we are, look.

He hands the paper to Matron. They all cluster round

Front page.
Matron (*reading*) "Hospital Scandal ... Missing Bits ..."

Each character grabs the paper for his or her line

Crisp "Uproar in hospital as patients tell all."
Jim "Patients' personal private parts pinched ..."
Crisp "I felt no pain–" (*pause*) "—only inconvenience."
Matron How horrible.
Bright You realize what this means?
Boldly No, Susan.
Bright It means—that whoever was responsible for the dodgy doings at St Hilary's, could now be on the run in St Sennapod's!
Crisp How ghastly!
Jim Nothing is safe!

George and Doris look beneath the sheets to check their bits, they breathe a sigh of relief. Lint snaps the case together and they all jump

Lint Sorry, Matron. May I make a suggestion? That everyone returns to their normal duties and the details of this strange incident are kept strictly within these four walls. Matron and I will deal with this matter. Is that agreed?
All Certainly. Absolutely right. We leave it to you.

The others exit, ad-libbing

Matron Mr Flower.
George Yes Matron!
Matron Mrs Bucket.
Doris Yes Matron!
Matron Take your sleeping and strengthening tablets please.
George
Doris } (*together*) Straight away, Matron.

Matron and Lint exit

As they do, Doris and George in unison take their tablets and zonk out. There is a pause then ...

George Chocolate finger? (*He passes it across*)
Doris Ta. (*She takes it*)

They appear to be asleep

Jim enters and comes downstage to speak to the audience

Jim I'm really worried about all these missing bits. I mean it could be us next. I think that creepy Dr Scalpel's got something to do with it, don't you?

They respond

Look, I know you've helped me so much already, getting ready for the party, curing the patients and all that, but do you think you could help me out again?

They respond

Really? Cor, ta very much. You see I've got this idea that old Scalpel and Tootski are nicking bits in the night and they must have some huge pair of scissors or snippers or something. Know what I mean? Somehow it must be able to snip bits off without you realizing. If you spot them with anything like that or if you see anything like it, could you give me a shout?

They respond

That's great! If you see it just shout "Jim, it's here!!!" This song'll help you to remember. We've got to catch them at it and find out how they're doing it.

Song 7: We've Got A Nasty Job To Do

(Singing)

We've got a nasty job to do
That's dangerous and dark
It's really up to all of us
To stop their little larks
We've got to catch those villains
We've got to sort 'em out
And 'ere's the way we'll do it
If you will help me out.

Any nipper that sees a snipper
Call me straight away
Any nipper that sniffs a snipper
Call me don't delay
Wave your arms
Clap your hands
Call out nice and clear
Any nipper that spots a snipper
Shout out . . .
"Jim it's here"

(Speaking) See you later and keep your eyes peeled!

Jim zips off as . . .

Matron and Lint creep in. Lint has the case of missing bits

Matron Well, Mr Lint, what kind of strategy do you suggest?
Lint Stealth!
Matron Stealth?
Lint I have a suspicion.
Matron Suspicion?
Lint Scalpel.
Matron Scalpel?
Lint St Hilary's Hospital.
Matron St Hilary's? Of course! That's where he and his abnormal assistant were practising . . .
Lint Practising . . . yes . . . but what, Matron?
Matron I follow your drift, Lint, but what's to be done?
Lint Return the case. Leave everything exactly as it was and use it as a trap.
Matron A trap to catch a rat.
Lint Scalpel is on duty with Crisp this evening and I believe he will strike tonight! (*Lint returns the case to the cupboard*)
Matron Then we must be here.
Lint What time?
Matron Ten to ten.
Lint Ten to ten—till then!

Lint and Matron exit

The stage darkens, and we realize that George and Doris are not really asleep

George Psst!

Doris What?

George Doris. You awake?

Doris Yea, I didn't take that sleeping pill.

George I didn't take those strength pills from my bottle either.

Doris Why?

George I didn't have enough strength to get the top off! There's too much funny business going on around here for my liking.

Doris You're right. I don't fancy waking up to find I've got vital bits missing.

George If you ask me, we're better off out of this loony bin and down the allotment.

Doris Yeah, but there's too many people coming in and out at the moment for us to make a run for it.

George Leave it till later, eh!

Doris Yes, about nine o'clock?

George No, even later, say ... er ...

Doris Ten to ten.

George OK, ten to ten.

Doris Till then.

They both zonk out. Pause

George Have another chocolate finger. (*He hands one to her*)

Doris Ta George, lovely.

They pretend to be asleep again. The Lights dim even further, mysterious music

Scalpel and Tootski enter. Tootski has a timetable on a piece of paper in her pocket

Scalpel Quickly, Tootski, don't dawdle. Zere is verk to be done.

Tootski I'm coming, I'm coming.

Scalpel Not so much noise unt kerfuffle.

Tootski Sorry.

Scalpel Now it is time ve started collecting schpecimens from St Sennapod's.

Tootski Eshpechially feet.

Scalpel I haven't forgotten my promise—you vill soon be complete.

Tootski Footloose und fancy free!

Scalpel If you insist. Have you ze timetable for duty staff?

Tootski (*handing it over*) Yes. You see your name is down for official duty tonight.

Scalpel (*reading it*) Vot's zis? (*He points to the bottom of the page*)

Tootski A footnote.

Scalpel Excellent. Ah, I see Miss Crisp is down to man ze svitchboard tonight.

Tootski She got nice feet.

Scalpel Feet schmeet! Let's take vone limb at a time, Tootski. First ve vill schnip a left mit.

Tootski Mit?

Scalpel Left hand.

Tootski Oh right.

Scalpel No left.

Tootski Right.

Scalpel Forget it. Have you got ze "schnipper"?

Tootski It's here. (*She collects the "snipper" from off-stage*)

Scalpel It's good. Check for efficiency.

Tootski One, two, three, "schnip".

Scalpel I like it. I like it, but too much noise for night-schnipping. Fit ze silencer.

Tootski Silencer fitted. (*She does so*)

The audience could well shout "Jim, it's here"

Scalpel Vot are zose stupid imbeciles shouting?

Tootski I never trusted them.

Jim (*off, shouting*) Coming!

Scalpel Quickly. I hear someone coming. It's zat stupid orderly.

Tootski He's got nice feet too!

Scalpel Shut up! This way!

They tear off with the snipper as ...

Jim dashes in from the other side

Jim (*breathless*) Did you see them?

The audience responds

Did they have anything with them?

Response

What's it like?

Response

It sounds 'orrible. Which way did they go?

They tell him

Right, thanks very much. Leave it all to me now. You've got to keep quiet otherwise they'll know we're on to them. OK? Right! I'll stop them if it's the last thing I do!!

Jim exits

Mysterious music and the Lights change to sinister blue as Crisp enters, nervously looks at the office, then makes her way to the switchboard

Doris and George make restless sleep noises—Crisp jumps

Crisp Oh my goodness, my nerves are in shreds. That dreadful business with the suitcase! My *feet* feel quite wobbly.

Tootski and Scalpel are now hidden near the switchboard

Tootski (*popping her head out excitedly at the prospect of feet*) Cor!
Crisp What was that? My imagination running riot again.

The audience may tell her

Be quiet. I don't want to be interrupted again. I must concentrate on the job in hand.
Scalpel (*head out, as above*) Cor!
Crisp Now let me see . . .

The Lights fade

Tomorrow's admissions.

Scalpel and Tootski meanwhile are preparing the "snipper"

Ah, only three in the morning. One—blocked nostril for surgery. Two—a rib replacement. Three—an ingrowing toenail.

The snipper opens ready to snip, but the switchboard buzzes

Scalpel Damn!

The snipper retracts

Crisp Hallo. . . . Yes. . . . You'd like tomorrow's duty rota? . . . Certainly. Just one moment while I get it . . .

She reaches out and sees the snipper opening. It snips, she screams and faints. Scalpel and Tootski cackle gleefully. The action and dialogue should now be delivered at a cracking pace

Scalpel Did you get it?
Tootski I don't know!
Scalpel Never mind, ze patients are vaking, bring ze schnipper, you fool!
Tootski Oh yes, zat vill be handy!
Scalpel Quick, under ze bed.

Scalpel and Tootski dive under the bed as George and Doris wake up

George Doris.
Doris What, George?
George It's ten to ten. Time to make a move.

They get out of bed

Doris Is the coast clear?
George Looks OK.
Doris Right, I'll just get my handbag. (*She reaches for her handbag but is disturbed by the noise of the "lovers" entering*)
Boldly (*off, calling*) Soooooosan!
Bright (*off, calling*) Steeephen!

George ⎫
Doris ⎪ (*together*) Damn!
Tootski ⎬
Scalpel ⎭
Doris Quick, under the beds, George!
George Right, Doris.
Doris Bit of a lark this, in'it.
George You can say that again.
Doris Bit of a lark this——
George Get under!!

They dive under the beds as Tootski and Scalpel roll out the other side of the bed and dive into Kipper's cubicle

   Boldly and Bright enter, and meet outside the cubicle

Boldly You came.
Bright I was alone.
Boldly I should've known.
Bright You were temptation!

They kiss. The snipper appears between the curtains of the cubicle

Boldly This is madness. I can't live without you, Susan.
Bright Oh Stephen. I'd give up everything for you.
Boldly You mean ...
Bright Yes, I'd even cut myself off——

The snipper is moving between them

   —from my nursing career.
Boldly Oh darling, then will you say ...
Bright Yes, Stephen. Yes, yes.

They are interrupted by the sounds of Matron and Lint

Matron (*whispering, off*) Lint!

The snipper zips back out of sight

Boldly Oh no! We mustn't be caught here in each other's arms, swept up in a whirlpool of crazed passion.
Lint (*whispering, off*) Over here, Matron!
Bright Quick, into the beds! There's someone coming.

Boldly and Bright each get into one of the beds

   Matron and Lint enter and meet in the environs of the office

Matron Lint, is the suitcase still in position?
Lint Yes, just as we left it.
Matron I'm convinced that that phoney Scalpel——

Scalpel quivers the cubicle curtains

   —and that overgrown foot, what's its name?
Lint Tootski.
Matron Yes Tootski, are at the bottom of this plot to corner the market in spare parts.
Lint I phoned St Hilary's and the descriptions match exactly.
Matron Good—now we need to catch them *red-handed*.
Lint With their pants down!
Matron There's no need to get carried away, Lint. All this excitement seems to have gone to your head.

The snipper moves out to Lint's head

Lint Well, Matron, I think it's a good job that I keep my ear to the ground.

The snipper hovers beside Lint's ear

   Jim enters UR *with Sir Barnaby. He spots the snipper as it is about to snip Lint's ear*

Jim Look out, Lint!

The snipper retracts. Everyone screams

Matron Stop them!
Lint Grab that snipper!

Tootski and Scalpel exit from the cubicle and head for the audience. They scream when they see the audience

Scalpel The window, quickly!
Tootski Wait for me, my foot!

Bright and Boldly sit up in bed clutching sheets and scream. Tootski and Scalpel turn and change direction towards the lift, as Crisp comes to. She sees them and screams

Crisp Aagh, where am I?
Scalpel Ze other vay.

They turn. As they do so, George grabs Scalpel and Doris grabs Tootski as they come out from under the beds. You might like a chase all over the auditorium

George Gotcher, you slimy snipper!

The Lights come up to normal

Scalpel Foiled!
Doris (*stamping on her foot*) Take that, freaky foot.
Tootski Ow! That's my corn!
Matron The tables are turned, Dr Scalpel.
Sir Barnaby The boot's on the other foot.
Crisp (*noticing Sir Barnaby*) I must be delirious, Sir Barnaby, is it really you?
Sir Barnaby Yes indeed it is.
Matron But Sir Barnaby, I thought you were missing . . .
Lint Presumed dead . . .
Matron That will do, thank you, Lint.
Jim I found him. These two (*pointing at Scalpel and Tootski*) were responsible for his disappearance.
Doris }
George } (*together*) Always suspected them, nasty bits of work.
Boldly What happened, sir? Damned disturbing.
Bright What did they do to you?
Sir Barnaby The scoundrels grabbed me as I was about to leave for my holiday, then bound and gagged, I was dumped down the dirty linen chute, and there I would almost certainly have expired, had it not been for the prompt action and rescue of young Jim Pill here.
Jim My pleasure and privilege, sir.
Boldly Good to have you back, sir. (*He puts his pipe back in his mouth*)
Bright (*looking at Boldly*) Damned good! (*She also has a pipe now*)
Boldly (*delighted*) Oh Susan.
Sir Barnaby Now get those two devils out of my sight. Detective Inspector Nab is waiting to deal with them in no uncertain manner.

Fred Bunch enters

Fred I certainly am, Sir Barnaby. These two have led me a merry old dance.
Jim But weren't you . . .?
Fred Making enquiries? Yes sir. And now I've tracked them down at last.
Sir Barnaby Put the cuffs on them, Inspector.
Fred Right, sir. (*He pulls out a broken bunch of daffodils*) Sorry about that, sir. Madam. (*He hands the flowers to Crisp*)
Crisp Oh Inspector, how charming.
Fred (*handcuffs ready*) Right, it's prison for you two and no funny business.
Scalpel Zere will be anuzzer time and anuzzer place, Sir Barnacles. In prison we will have more time to zink unt plan more devilish schemes. Eh Tootski?
Tootski I'll be able to put my feet up.
Scalpel Shut up, you fool.
Doris }
George } (*together*) Come on, you two. (*They grab them*)
Fred No more nickin' bits in the night.
All Right!

Doris, George, Fred and Jim exit with Scalpel and Tootski under arrest

Crisp And now you're back, Sir Barnaby, I hope and trust that the hospital can return to some normality.
Sir Barnaby I hope so, Miss Crisp, I sincerely hope so.
Crisp Well, I'll start by making some coffee.

She exits

Matron (*spotting Boldly and Bright in bed*) I don't wish to appear personal, Dr Boldly, but just what do you and Nurse Bright think you are doing in that most unprofessional position?

Lint In bed. (*Gloating*) Together.

Matron Thank you, Lint, I can see quite clearly.

Boldly Gosh, sorry, Matron.

They both get out

It's not as bad as it seems. Nurse Bright and I are getting hitched.

Bright Engaged.

Matron ⎫
⎬ (*together*) What!
Lint ⎭

Bright To be married.

Boldly To each other.

Sir Barnaby Congratulations, Boldly, and you too, Bright. (*He shakes their hands*) Tell you what, I shan't be using these two holiday tickets now, maybe you could find some use for them?

Boldly I say, sir, that's most awfully generous.

Bright Damned generous!

Lint We can't possibly allow this, Matron!

Bright (*appealing*) Matron?

Matron (*relenting slightly, smiling*) Well, what are you waiting for?

Boldly You mean ... Oh thank you, Matron. Goodbye all. Coming, Susie?

Bright (*producing a hidden case*) I'm packed already.

Boldly Gosh!

Lint Nauseating!

Boldly and Bright exit

Matron Well, let us hope that that was the last surprise of the night.

There is a cacophany of sound off-stage. Buckets clanging, screams, etc. George enters with his foot stuck in a fire bucket and Doris enters with a watering can stuck on her head. Crisp enters with coffee and Jim. She puts the tray on the table

Crisp (*as she spots them*) Oh no!

Matron It seems I was wrong.

Jim (*despairing*) Don't ask me how it happened, it just did.

There is a caterwauling of a newborn child in the cubicle (baby noises can be made by cast members)

Sir Barnaby What now!

Kenneth Kipper appears with his wife, Nurse Cuddle, and small baby. It has a little kipper sticking out of its mouth, and is beaming, they are proud parents

It's our first little kipper.

Baby Goo goo. (*Baby noises can be made by one of the cast*)

Matron Lint! Call Maternity!

Lint Maternity!

The rest of the Company rush on with bottles, drip feeds etc., making a colossal noise. A midwife enters on a tricycle. She stops baby crying when a feeding bottle is supplied

Jim The baby's arrived just in time for the party. 'Ere, wot's her name?

Cuddle We'd like to call her Dolores after Miss Crisp.

Crisp Well of course I'd be most flattered.

All Good old Crispy!

Crisp Well what an exciting day it's been and what a happy ending. Most of it due to Jim and all of you out there—so I'd just like to say ...

Song 8: Thank You Everyone (a round)

Jim
Thank you thank you everyone
We hope you all enjoyed the fun
Thank you for helping, you're our mates
Have a lovely party, 'cos we think you're great!

Reprise as a round. At the end of the song, balloons float down etc.

CURTAIN

Note: At the end of the show you might like to have the lucky number draw and hand out balloons and/or small gifts. Say goodbye to the audience at the door. Tootski and Scalpel under police escort of course.

FURNITURE AND PROPERTY LIST

ACT I

In auditorium: Decorations, balloons, etc.

On stage: 2 hospital beds with pillows, sheets, blankets
On Doris's bed: bra, knickers under blanket (for Fred page 8), temperature chart at end, radio headphones at top, surgical mask under pillow
On George's bed: bedtray over bed, temperature chart at end, radio headphones at top; flowers in pots, tools, seed packets, labels, stickers under bed; surgical mask under pillow
2 bedside lockers. *On Doris's:* bowl of grapes
2 bed screens
Pulley hoist next to Doris's bed
Corner cupboard
Window curtains
Cubicle with curtains, marked EMERGENCY ADMISSIONS. *Behind rear curtain or doorway:* wallpaper, paste, brushes (some walls can already be decorated in the same paper, or rolls can be dropped from above so that walls appear to be decorated by Kipper (page 10); kettle full of water, teapot (page 10); small table and chair, meal on a plate, cutlery, 2 cups and saucers, tablecloth (page 13); small TV, standard lamp (both practical), pictures for wall (nails already in place on flats) (page 18); cardboard heart (page 18)
Filing cabinet. *In it:* folders
Table. *On it:* switchboard, telephone, 3 folders containing 3 admission forms, rubber stamp and pad, small standing mirror, files, large lidded box containing pens, small sign MISS CRISP—RECEPTION
Swivel chair
Sign—RECEPTION AREA
Low table. *On it:* paper, pencils
4 chairs
Lift with sliding door and bell or glockenspeil
Signs on walls—EXIT, EMERGENCY EXIT, WARD 12 THIS WAY, WARD 10, etc.

Off stage: Suitcase marked "British Airways", "Virgin Islands" and other holiday labels, bucket and spade (**Sir Barnaby**)
Medical book, pencil (**Cuddle**)
Bunch of daffodils (**Fred**)
Overnight bag (**Kipper**)
Overnight bag containing male clothes (**Doris**)
Overnight bag containing female clothes (**George**)
2 counterpanes (**Jim**)
Surgical bowl (**Jim**)
Clipboard (**Lint**)
Flippers, snorkel, large hypodermic filled with water (**Sir Barnaby**)
Very bedraggled bunch of daffodils, bandages on head and fingers (**Fred**)
Trolley covered with sheet with hole (**Bright**)
Very bedraggled bunch of daffodils (**Fred**)
Huge hypodermic (**Bright**)
Trolley covered with large sheet with hole. *On shelf beneath:* rubber gloves, scissors, garden shears, scalpel, surgical equipment. *Under sheet:* sausages, teddy bears, kettles, etc. (**Jim**)
Suitcase, huge carving knife (**Scalpel**)

Personal: **Miss Crisp**: glasses on string, pen on string round neck
Lint: biros in top pocket, clipboard, wrist-watch, pebble glasses, rubber gloves in pocket
Sir Barnaby: monocle, large key
Boldly: wrist-watch, pipe, heavy-framed glasses
Bright: hypodermic, prop tonsils
Matron: watch, deodorant spray
Kipper: rubber or plastic kipper tail protruding from mouth
Doris: bucket stuck on foot
George: watering can containing water stuck on head
Jim: diary in pocket

Tootski: fake foot, arm sling with concealed hammer
All: knives, industrial tools for Song 3: Anthem to Sir Barnaby; gowns, masks, concealed party hats, streamers and poppers for operation

ACT II

Set: Suitcase containing a variety of missing bits—a horrible hand, a festered foot, a nobbly nose, a fishy finger, a severed scalp, bits of bone in a tin, amputated ear'oles; knife, card for Scalpel
Newspaper on reception table
Gooseberries, castanets, chocolate fingers under George's pillow
Blood-pressure kit with balloon attached, handbag in Doris's locker
Bottle of sleeping pills, glass of water on Doris's locker
Castanets, pin (to burst balloon) under Doris's pillow
Bottle of strength pills, glass of water on George's locker
Bright's suitcase with JUST MARRIED on it under Doris's bed
Balloon net above stage

Off stage: Trolley (**Jim, Bright**)—optional
Watering can (**George**)
Bucket (**Doris**)
Pile of sheets (**Bright**)
Case of missing bits (**Jim**)
Pile of files (**Matron, Lint**)
Case of missing bits (**Lint**)
Snipper, silencer (**Tootski**)
Tray with cups of coffee (**Crisp**)
Baby in swaddling clothes with small kipper (**Cuddle**)
Tricycle with sign attached MATERNITY, bottles, drip feeds (**Nurses**)

Personal: **Cuddle**: wedding veil, posy
Kipper: topper
Vicar: bible, confetti
Tootski: key on string in fake foot, timetable in pocket
Boldly: pipe, glasses, reflex rubber hammer
Bright: pipe in pocket
Fred: broken bunch of daffodils in pocket, handcuffs
Sir Barnaby: monocle, holiday tickets in pocket
Doris: watering can stuck on head for finale
George: fire bucket stuck on foot for finale

LIGHTING PLOT

Practical fittings required: standard lamp, TV

Interior. A hospital ward. The same scene throughout

ACT I

To open:	Bright, general interior lighting	
Cue 1	**Boldly** clicks his fingers *Sudden dim to romantic pink*	(Page 9)
Cue 2	**George** clicks his fingers *Return to previous lighting*	(Page 9)
Cue 3	**Boldly** clicks his fingers *Repeat Cue 1*	(Page 9)
Cue 4	As Song 2 ends *Return to previous lighting*	(Page 10)
Cue 5	**Sir Barnaby** enters *Follow spot on him*	(Page 12)
Cue 6	**Sir Barnaby** exits *Cut follow spot*	(Page 12)
Cue 7	**Matron** and **Lint** exit *Fade lights slightly*	(Page 14)
Cue 8	**Scalpel** and **Tootski** exit *Increase lighting*	(Page 15)
Cue 9	**Matron**: ". . . we-are-ready-for-you." *Dim lights*	(Page 15)
Cue 10	When trolley is in position *Bright downward spot on trolley and* **Fred**	(Page 15)
Cue 11	**Boldly** (*singing*): "And stitched 'em neatly." *Dim to lighting concentrated on* **Boldly**	(Page 16)
Cue 12	**Boldly** finds gloves and holds them up *Increase to general lighting*	(Page 17)
Cue 13	**Crisp**: ". . . knows what they're doing." *Snap on TV effect and standard lamp in cubicle*	(Page 18)
Cue 14	**Tootski** screams as case drops on foot; all freeze *Black-out*	(Page 19)

ACT II

To open:	Bright, general lighting	
Cue 15	**Bright** and **Boldly** exit *Fade lights on reception area, leaving pool of light on beds*	(Page 23)
Cue 16	**Doris** and **George** dive under covers *Return to general lighting*	(Page 24)
Cue 17	**Lint**: "Ten to ten—till then!" *Fade lighting*	(Page 27)
Cue 18	**Doris** and **George** pretend to be asleep again *Fade lighting further*	(Page 28)
Cue 19	**Jim**: ". . . the last thing I do!" *Sinister blue lighting*	(Page 29)

Cue 20   **Crisp**: "Now let me see ..."   (Page 29)
                Fade lights

Cue 21   **George**: "Gotcher, you slimy snipper!"   (Page 31)
                Lights come up again

EFFECTS PLOT

ACT I

Cue 1   When Company have assembled on stage   (Page 1)
Switchboard buzzer

Cue 2   **Fred** exits   (Page 8)
Repeat Cue 1

Cue 3   **Crisp**: "... or what's left of them."   (Page 8)
Repeat Cue 1

Cue 4   **Crisp's** bottom bumps against switchboard   (Page 9)
Repeat Cue 1

Cue 5   **Tootski** hits **Fred** with hammer   (Page 15)
Loud pop

Cue 6   When trolley is in position   (Page 16)
Bring up heavy breathing, heartbeats, electrical operation sounds

Cue 7   **Boldly** raises his hands   (Page 16)
Cut noises

Cue 8   **Boldly** exits   (Page 18)
Repeat Cue 1

Cue 9   **Kipper** places cardboard heart between himself and **Cuddle**   (Page 18)
Bell-like ding

ACT II

Cue 10   **Boldly** and **Scalpel** shake hands   (Page 22)
Huge crunching sound

Cue 11   **Crisp**: "... an ingrowing toenail." Snipper opens ready   (Page 29)
Repeat Cue 1

Cue 12   At end of Song 8   (Page 32)
Release balloon net

TICKETS

ST. SENNAPOD'S HOSPITAL

Appointment card to see

Surgical Sensation at St. Sennapod's

Please fill in and hand to Matron
or Administrator upon arrival

NAME:

ADDRESS:

BOY/GIRL (delete one) Lucky number ......

ADMISSIONS FORM

NAME . . . .

ADDRESS . . . .

NEXT OF KIN . . . .

SEX . . . .

ARE YOU MISSING ANY BITS? . . . .

HAVE YOU HAD ANY OF THE FOLLOWING
  'ORRIBLE DISEASES? . . . .

CAN YOU GIVE BLOOD?
  MINIMUM DONATION SIX BUCKETS . . . .

WHAT COLOUR ARE YOUR PYJAMAS? . . . .

WOULD YOU OBJECT TO SHARING A BED? . . . .

DO YOU MIND A LITTLE PAIN? . . . .

HAVE YOU BROUGHT ANY SANDWICHES? . . . .

WHAT KIND? . . . .

    Sir B B Barrington
    St. Sennapod's Hospital

TOOTSKI'S FOOT

SHOE GLUED TO PLYWOOD
SOLE 17 IN. LONG.

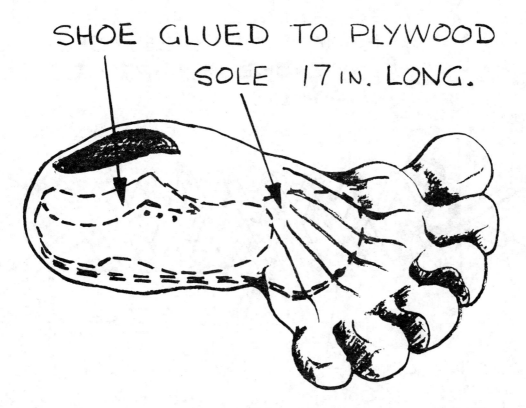

BUILD UP FOOT SHAPE 22 IN.
LONG BY GLUING ON PIECES OF
PLASTIC SPONGE, AIDED BY
MASKING TAPE WRAPPED ROUND
IN PLACES TO PULL IT INTO SHAPE.
COVER WITH STOCKINETTE OR
SIMILAR. PAINT TO LOOK
GRUESOME — NUMBER OF TOES
OPTIONAL.

SNIPPERS

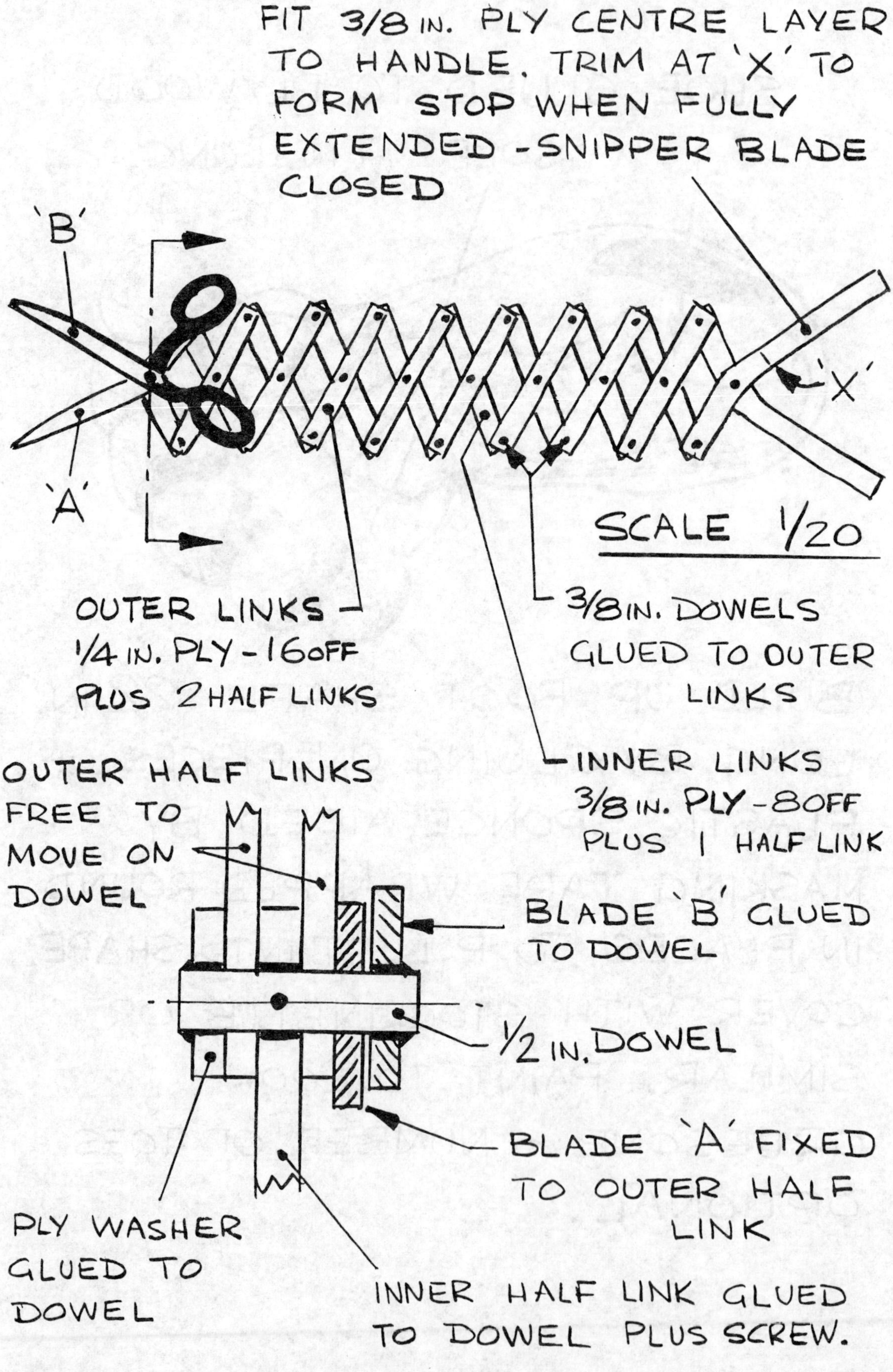

FIT 3/8 IN. PLY CENTRE LAYER
TO HANDLE. TRIM AT 'X' TO
FORM STOP WHEN FULLY
EXTENDED - SNIPPER BLADE
CLOSED

'B'

'A'

'X'

SCALE 1/20

OUTER LINKS
1/4 IN. PLY - 16 OFF
PLUS 2 HALF LINKS

3/8 IN. DOWELS
GLUED TO OUTER
LINKS

INNER LINKS
3/8 IN. PLY - 8 OFF
PLUS 1 HALF LINK

OUTER HALF LINKS
FREE TO
MOVE ON
DOWEL

BLADE 'B' GLUED
TO DOWEL

1/2 IN. DOWEL

BLADE 'A' FIXED
TO OUTER HALF
LINK

PLY WASHER
GLUED TO
DOWEL

INNER HALF LINK GLUED
TO DOWEL PLUS SCREW.

ST. SENNAPOD'S AT YOUR SERVICE

Repeat the last 4 bars then
repeat the whole thing for other
verses.

ANTHEM TO SIR BARNABY

Arr. S.R.P.

TUESDAY, TONSILS AND YOU

NICKIN' BITS IN THE NIGHT

An J.R.P.

I'VE LEFT MY GLOVES IN

ALL   WHEN THERE WERE DOUBTS   I TOOK THE   PLUNGE   CUT BIG LUMPS

OUT—   I FACED IT ALL   AND I   STOOD   TALL   AND STUCK 'EM NEATLY —.

SEE TEXT FOR
VERSE TWO.

Arr. J.R.P.

COME TO MY 'LOTMENT

Repeat three times using verses two and three.   Arr. I.R.P.

WE'VE GOT A NASTY JOB TO DO

THANK YOU EVERYONE

MADE AND PRINTED IN GREAT BRITAIN BY
LATIMER TREND & COMPANY LTD PLYMOUTH

MADE IN ENGLAND

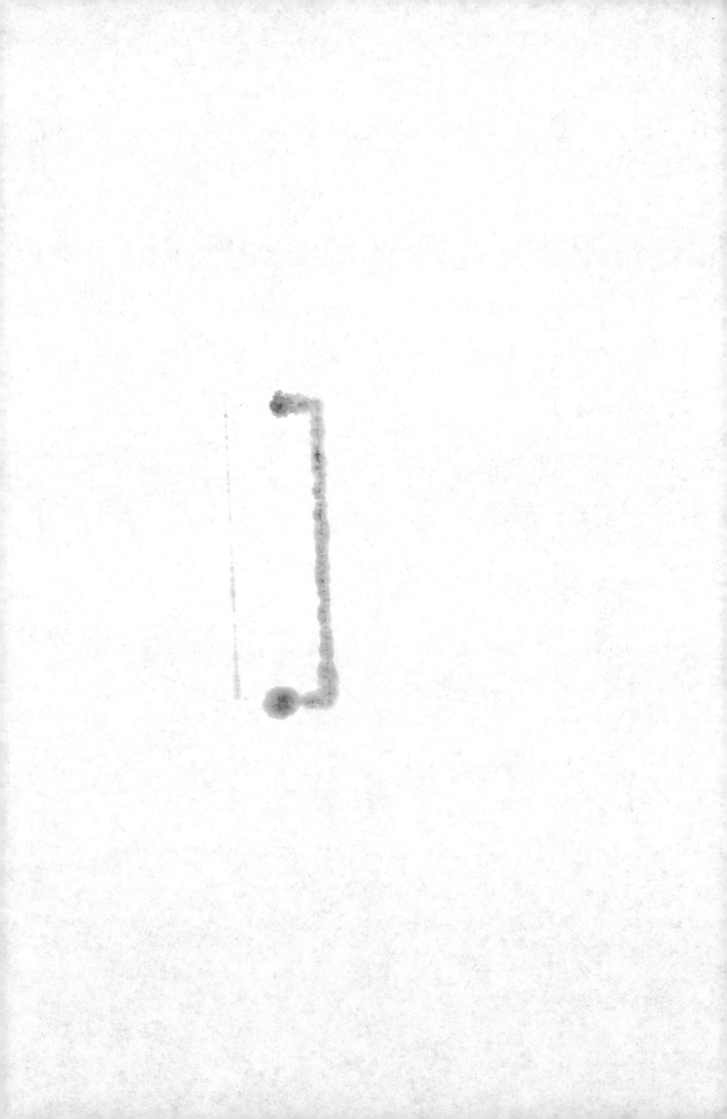